HAUNTED
BRAY
& ENVIRONS

Charleville House, Enniskerry.

HAUNTED
BRAY
& ENVIRONS

Eddie Tynan

The
History
Press
Ireland

For Richard
Through thick and thin

First published 2010

The History Press Ireland
119 Lower Baggot Street
Dublin 2
Ireland

www.thehistorypress.ie

© Eddie Tynan, 2010

The right of Eddie Tynan to be identified as the Author
of this work has been asserted in accordance with the
Copyrights, Designs and Patents Act 1988.

ISBN 978 1 8455 5995 1
Typesetting and origination by The History Press
Printed in Great Britain

Contents

Introduction

As a native of Bray, I have always been fascinated by accounts I have heard over the years of alleged paranormal events in Bray and its surroundings. I have decided to collect these accounts in the hope that they will be of general interest and also to preserve them before they disappear from human memory.

The study of the paranormal has for centuries taxed the minds of many. Documented accounts have been recorded in almost every country on the planet for the past 1,000 years. The study of these phenomena is not and can never be an exact science; it is and has always been too open-ended and prone to deception. Paradoxically the older the case, the more reliable is its source. Among the many who have made a life study of these phenomena, one leading expert of world renown, Fr Herbert Thurston S.J., summed up this whole dilemma in the following words:

That there may be something diabolical, or at any rate evil, in them I do not deny. But on the other hand, it is also possible that there may be natural forces involved which are so far as little known to us as the latent forces of electricity were known to the Greeks. It is possibly the complication of these two elements which forms the heart of the mystery.

one

A Tale of Possession

On the morning of 3 October in the last year of the nineteenth century, there was a burial in the old graveyard on the Powerscourt estate in the County of Wicklow that was to reawaken a tale that had been heard in our village and surrounding districts for generations. It was the story of Pamela Ingram. I was the one to open her grave after sixty years and had curiosity not got the better of me, it would have ended there. After I had unravelled the few threads of information I remembered hearing as a boy, my search led me to Queenie Doyle in Ballyray and the diary of Fr Byrne, which fate or providence put in my hands. I've often regretted my actions for they've brought neither mental nor monetary reward, only years of preoccupation with matters that bear no resemblance to everyday life, something better left alone or, at least, in the hands of those qualified to understand them. Paradoxically, I have written this account as much to be rid of its burden as to share it.

I am Joseph O'Toole, son of James O'Toole and Mary Furlong. My ancestors held these lands until the soldiers came and drove us out. The Powerscourts built their house on the site of our castle, which had stood there for centuries.

So began for them the first creation, the flowering of Anglo-Protestantism, which was to bloom for one hundred years. The merchants of Dublin would make our capital the second city of the

Empire. The old Gaelic order was swept away. The wealthy built their town houses, Powerscourts' comprising over a hundred rooms. It was against this background of power and opulence that Pamela Ingram first made her appearance. Who she was and where she came from became a talking point in society. Some said she was the offspring of the King of Spain's brother, while others whispered that she was the offspring of mad George of England. She, for her part, remained tight-lipped on the subject, indifferent to gossip that, from the start, was to give her an air of mystery. One thing all were agreed upon: never had a more beautiful creature been seen in the kingdom.

The Powerscourts took her to themselves, beginning the season with a ball in her honour, which was held at their stately home. At one point in the evening, forty admirers were listed to dance with her and wives were seen to keep more than a vigilant eye on husbands. She was under constant scrutiny – a barrage of lorgnettes scanning her every feature. Pockets of local girls converged in the corner of the ballroom, spite and agitation written on their faces as they beheld the spectacle of eligible young men from the district, like panting dogs, waiting their turn for a dance. Lord Burton's youngest daughter fled the room in hysterics when her fiancé took the floor with Pamela, fearing she had lost him for good. After the ball, servants were barraged with requests for basins of hot water and salts to be sent to the gentlemen's rooms to ease feet and ankles after the rigors of the dance floor. It was all a great success. Lady Pike, who was considered an authority on such matters, rendered the final verdict: Lady Pamela was the revelation of the season – a verdict unanimously agreed on by the society papers which had covered the event. Her address book was full for the season, with ten proposals of marriage, eight of which, it was said, were from married men.

Next morning, sitting at breakfast, having winded his Lordship's best bay mare with her gallops over his demesne, her wit and charm captivated all. She was not without her detractors; her origin would continue to be a talking point in many quarters of society.

The Powerscourts could not bear to have her out of their sight. A special wing of the house was furnished for her. Her days were a mad whirl of

excitement; every night a ball was held somewhere in her
Dublin society finally stopped to catch its breath it kne╵
its new leader. It was a position she would hold for many
walking a tightrope between respectability and the many
more sinister rumours that were starting to circulate about ner.

Society was agog when news finally leaked out of her impending
marriage to Lord Ingram, sixty years her senior and immensely rich. The
papers had a field day depicting Ingram as blind, deaf and doddering.
One Dublin wit dubbed the relationship, 'spring in the lap of winter'.
She was furious at her tormentors, stating, 'Though somewhat advanced
in years, Lord Ingram is the epitome of all that a gentleman should be
and is in full possession of his faculties,' which made her name a byword
for laughter in every salon in Dublin. Some time later, it was announced
in the papers that they were to be married. Dublin society prepared itself
for the event of the year.

❈ ❈ ❈

Powerscourt House had been a hive of activity for weeks, with special
chefs being brought over from Paris; scores of maids and footmen were
installed. Two marquees were erected on the lawn to assist the overflow.
Anybody who was anybody was there; the Lord Lieutenant and his wife,
and all of the dignitaries of Dublin Castle were present. Lord Powerscourt
had his workers erect a marquee next to the village in which his tenants
could celebrate the joyous occasion. Every night there was music and
dancing, with people coming from Bray and Newtown. Pipers and
fiddlers found their way to our village and there wasn't a sober man to
be seen for a week. The young folk had a rare time scuttling after the
coaches that came and went daily, carefully avoiding the whips, which
were frequently used to dislodge them. On the morning of the wedding,
our village witnessed a constant procession of coaches, which made their
way up to Powerscourt House. As old Matt Byrne said as he spit after
them, 'Cromwell's vermin'. The *Freeman's Journal*, who covered the event,
were far more discreet!

Powerscourt House, Enniskerry c.1910.

The weather proved disappointing, with bursts of sunshine through intermittent showers. The couple was married in the little church next to Powerscourt House. The altar and walls had been arranged with every conceivable species of flowers. As Pamela walked up the aisle, she presented a figure of indescribable beauty, compared with the ogre who walked by her side. There were remarks made of 'Oh shame!' as they walked to the altar. A gasp of astonishment rang through the church when, at the exchange of the marriage vows, it was revealed that she was a Montague, descended from one of the great families of England. Only the very uninformed were surprised by this revelation. Old Lady Hardwick had spent much time searching her origins back to the Montagues. It transpired that an uncle had reared her. Society was strict in such matters and only those who could prove their credentials could enter its portals: any hint of scandal, and it closed ranks. When her uncle died, he left her his title and fortune, making her a wealthy woman in her own right. She had spent years on the continent, gaining knowledge in the arts and sciences and the new philosophies that were taking Europe by storm.

She was twenty when she entered Dublin society. Forty years later, there were people who would swear that she hadn't aged a day.

The sun was shining when they made their way from the church and the short distance to Powerscourt House and the banquet that awaited them, which was to last for a week. Ingram, after two glasses of champagne, fell asleep and was taken home to his bed without his bride, which caused many a frown from the ladies. The gentlemen, on the other hand, were delighted. The absence of young Lord Derby was much deplored. He had travelled from London to attend the wedding. It was universally known that he was madly in love with Pamela. It later transpired that when he beheld the sight of his love walking up the aisle with Ingram he had to be restrained. He dashed around the side of the church and attempted to hang himself from a yew tree with his own cravat. Though luckily caught in time, he never recovered from the shock and died shortly after. When Pamela was told of this, she was to display a coldness of heart that shocked many, with her remark, 'How romantic, it should delight in the retelling.'

With the festivities finally over, Pamela Montague, now Lady Pamela Ingram, moved into Charleville House, her rooms within sight of Powerscourt House. She continued to live as she had up to then, with a never-ending round of dinner parties and balls, without the company of Ingram, who seemed content to sit by his fireside and read. She considered Charleville too small and out of the way. She moved to her town house in Dublin where she would spend weeks at a time, only then returning to her country seat. Ingram died within a year of the marriage and was buried in Powerscourt cemetery, not twenty feet from where he had stood on his wedding day. He left his wife one of the wealthiest women in the kingdom, with estates in England and Europe. Not long after Ingram's death she closed Charleville and moved to the continent.

All manner of scandal filtered back to Ireland. The London papers had her romantically connected to some of the most eligible gentlemen in

and some of the most disreputable. London and Dublin society
th each other for the smallest titbits of gossip. She was not without
..... es. One paper quoted, 'Lady Pamela Ingram is not only larger than
life, but larger than the many lies that have been told about her.' Every
year she returned for the Dublin season, always with a different partner,
usually a foreigner. All was forgiven. One look at her dazzling beauty
and it was impossible to believe the things that were spoken about her.
Her zest and appetite for life invigorated everyone who came in contact
with her. The mighty of the land vied with one another to have her at
their dinner parties, which, without her, were dismal failures. Hers was
the most improbable of lives; she had everything she could desire, but
behind the glamour, she longed for a meaningful life, to marry and have
children. It was said that Ingram's will had made this impossible. If she
were to do so, she would lose every penny of the vast inheritance he had
left her. To the world she represented everything that was wonderful and
exciting, hers the perfect life. In the intervening years, a new generation
would discover her. She would dance and flirt with the sons of men
she had danced and flirted with forty years before, when the dullards
and cowards as she called them, had returned to their estates, married
dutiful wives, and taken up politics or gardening, or both. She was still to
be seen at the best houses, laughing at the follies of her age, always the
impeccable guest, written and spoken about wherever she went.

There were those who long considered her dangerous to know. As
the years passed, it became harder to resist the many scandals that were
told of her, of the broken lives she had left in her wake. The Hardwicks
went to the wall after years of constant entertainment. Hardwick had
shot himself in his study rather than face the shame of the bankruptcy
courts. There were stories of suicides and broken marriages, which to
many, especially the young, only added to her appeal, her aura of danger.
In a society that was changing, she represented everything that belonged
to a more romantic age. Many of the beauties of her youth were now old
matrons, seldom seen in society. Some had taken to their rooms; many
had sought reparation for the follies of their youth in charitable works,
yet she stood resplendent, a symbol of an age that was ending.

Who and what was she? From the salons of Paris to the highest houses in the land, her name was spoken. Many believed she had made a pact with the devil for eternal youth. She would continue for many years to be the most sought after and talked about woman of her time.

Then suddenly, she was yesterday's news, the papers no longer wrote of her, the young no longer mouthed her sayings nor aped her manners. To the world she was dead. Society with its cold heart discarded her; it had found new toys to play with. The age of Pamela Ingram was over.

Twenty years later, a coach entered our village and made its way past Mr Grattan's house at Tinahinch, over the old bridge and up the avenue to Charleville House. Rumours spread that one of the old women in the village caught sight of the person in the carriage – it was Lady Pamela Ingram, though barely recognisable. She was now an old woman with snow-white hair. The village was alive with the gossip. The widow Cullen said they'd all be better employed tending to their own needs, instead of watching the coming and goings of their betters.

The rumour proved to be true: Pamela Ingram had returned to Charleville, her country seat. There were many discussions about the reasons she had returned there after so many years abroad, when she could be living in the grand manner in Paris or London. It was commonly believed that she had come home to die. From the day that she set foot in Charleville, she was never seen again.

Over the years, stories were told about that place and its lonely inhabitant. Nobody in our village was ever employed by her. All wines and provisions came from Dublin. A young foreign lad whom she had brought with her was her only servant and companion.

After the gossip had settled down, life took on its usual round of drudgery. The young people of the village paid no heed to the stories told about her. In time, everyone forgot about the old lady living in our midst.

One morning, news of her death spread through the village. The papers gave the obituary. Her remains were to be interred in the old graveyard in Powerscourt. At eleven o'clock the following morning, the hearse carrying her remains arrived at the cemetery gate, followed by a coach carrying the vicar and the young foreign lad, now a handsome young man. Four of Lord Powerscourt's workmen had to be summoned to carry the coffin to the graveside. After a short service they all departed. My father was the gravedigger for the parish and it was he who buried Pamela Ingram. No headstone was ever erected over her grave. Over the years it became covered with briars. There was nothing to indicate that Pamela Ingram had ever lived.

There was talk in the village as to why none of the local gentry had attended the service and why she had not been buried with Ingram. Not long after, an agent came from London. The gardeners were paid off and the gates of Charleville House were locked. The house was then put up for sale.

It seems like yesterday that the Revd Odlum came to my house and informed me that Lady Pamela Ingram's grave was to be reopened. A coffin would arrive at Bray Station that evening and be brought to the church. Interment would take place the following morning at eleven. Revd Odlum informed me that they were the remains of an old foreign gentleman whom, years before, Pamela Ingram had brought from the continent to live with her at Charleville House. His last request was to be buried with his lady.

That afternoon, I opened the lock on the cemetery gate and walked the short distance to the old church. It was now a ruin, long since vacated when the parish had grown and moved to St Patrick's, near our village. I sat, lit my pipe and gazed at the scene before me. It was a melancholy sight. Many of the graves were covered with briar and ivy. Luckily I had a good idea of where to look for her grave, as my father had often pointed it out to me. I found her grave next to Ingram's and began to dig, having first hacked away the briars. Burying the pick in the earth, I heard a thud. Not realising how far down I had gone, I had penetrated the coffin lid and when I brought the pick up, the lid had come away. I was gazing at the remains of what was once Pamela Ingram. There was a cross in the coffin. Its position indicated that it had once been in her hands. I found this strange, knowing from experience that it was not a ritual that the Protestant Church indulged. I put the coffin lid back, and made my way home.

The next morning we laid the coffin in the earth next to Pamela Ingram. Revd Odlum lead the service, then all departed, leaving me to fill in the grave.

It was later that I began to think of the stories that I had heard when I was a lad – men trapping rabbits at night, hearing cries coming from her rooms in Charleville, of an ungodly relationship between her and her young servant, who was rumoured to be her son. Stories we young ones laughed at but we were careful never to venture near that place. I resolved to make some inquiries. I was at a distinct disadvantage as all who would have known anything were long since dead. There were names I remembered – Bessie Doyle, housekeeper to Fr Byrne, and then there was the widow Cullen, who stopped going to Mass after the coming of the electricity. The reason being, she said, that since God has given mankind this marvel of science, there hadn't been a banshee or a chord of fairy music heard in the district, that it was all pishrogery and lies invented by the clergy to keep us in our place.

Bessie Doyle's niece Queenie lived in Ballyray, near Powerscourt waterfall. I decided to visit her. I would often regret the hour I had done so. She lived alone. Over a cup of tea one evening she told me stories about the old folk she remembered as a child, also stories told to her by her aunt who had been Fr Byrne's housekeeper for years. When I asked her about Charleville House, and whether she had heard any stories concerning it, she went quiet and, try as I might, I couldn't get another word out of her on the subject.

When it was time to leave, she quietly went into the back room and brought back what appeared to me to be a bible. It had belonged to her aunt, she said. It had lain in a box with other books in a corner of Fr Byrne's presbytery. When he died, the new parish priest, eager to put his own stamp on the place had it completely redecorated. It was he who had given the books to her aunt. Bessie told me that years before, she had read part of the book she now had in her hand. She had been frightened by its contents and was unable to sleep nights. She handed the book to me. I left soon after, promising to return it. She seemed frightened again and told me to keep it. Bessie was a simple soul and I paid little heed to what she had said. I was disappointed that she was so reluctant to talk about Charleville House.

It was dark as I passed Powerscourt House, down the front avenue, and home. I made myself a mug of tea, settled in a chair, and opened the book. At five the following morning, I left it down, dazed and shaken. It was not a book, but a diary written by Fr Byrne sixty years before. The first part of it was delightful. It dealt with the life of our village all those years ago. There were names of people I remembered my father speaking of, records of marriages, baptisms, death, the joys and sorrows of your average village. It was only when I was halfway through it that I began to read words like demons and exorcism. I realised that I had read Fr Byrne's account of an exorcism, so terrifying that it beggared belief. It resembled more the ravings of a mad man than the account of one who was still remembered with pride in our parish.

I got over the initial shock by convincing myself that what I had read was the dialogue of a play. It was probably a defense that my mind had put up to shield me from what I felt, deep down, to be the truth. Though far from being a scholar, I had some book learning to my credit and I considered myself as intelligent as the next man, but this was something that I couldn't settle by sheer logic alone. It seemed too absurd. This was my village, where all belonging to me had lived for generations. I knew Charleville House and had walked its fields and woods. Could that beautiful place have been the scene of a visitation by Satan, where in one of its rooms, two priests had wrestled for the soul of Pamela Ingram? A part of me laughed at the improbability of it all. The only reality I knew was that Pamela Ingram was not a figment of the imagination.

That she died at Charleville House was beyond dispute – my father had buried her. Sixty years later I would reopen her grave to receive the remains of what was her foreign servant, though rumoured to be her son. Why was she never buried with Ingram? Why no monument to her memory? Why had nobody attended her funeral? Why were the last years of her life so shrouded in mystery? I decided to find out as much as I could about her life. I took journeys to the city of Dublin to scrutinise the papers of the period. I began to build up a picture of her in my mind. Sifting through musty newspapers, then seeing in my mind's eye the remains in the coffin I had unwittingly opened, reminded me of the vanity of all things! This was a woman who even by the standards of her time stood head and shoulders over the most decadent of her age. There was the vexing question of why Fr Byrne would have left a diary of such importance lying around instead of having it locked away. I had intended going to the Jesuit Order and inquiring of them if there ever had been a Fr Fennell in their ranks, a name that is repeatedly mentioned in the diaries. After months of research I made a decision to drop all future inquiry. I had become obsessed and was unable to go about my daily life. For years to come my dreams were haunted by what I had read in the diaries. I made a copy and returned the original to Queenie Doyle, urging her to be rid of it. What is written here is faithful to the original text. Nothing has been added in the slightest degree.

On a June night in the year 1840, Fr Byrne had an unexpected caller. It was a young foreign man. He told the priest that his lady was dying and had demanded to see a priest and that she was none other than Pamela Ingram of Charleville House. Fr Byrne questioned the young man as to the nature of her wanting to see a Catholic priest, knowing that she was not of that faith. But the young man was so insistent that, in the end, he relented. Some instinct told him that this was something out of the ordinary. He went to the tabernacle where he removed the Host and put it into a small casket, which he placed in his inside pocket. Filling a bottle of Holy Water from the font, he took his stole, surplice, and breviary, put on his overcoat, and walked to the waiting coach. They commenced the journey down past Tinahinch, over the old bridge, and up the avenue that led to Charleville House, a distance of a few miles.

When he entered the room, he was assailed by an indescribable stench. On the bed lay an old woman, bald-headed, her face bloodless. The eyes which stared at him held a look of terror and malignant hatred. He felt he was in the presence of some terrible evil. He was vaguely aware of such phenomena. Many years before, he had studied in France in preparation for his ordination. It was there he had spoken to a French priest who had performed an exorcism. Many of the younger, more progressive priests laughed at such stories. As children of the enlightenment, they considered such things a throwback to a more superstitious age. The Church had always taught that human beings could be possessed by demons. Each priest had in his breviary the rite of exorcism and could, at his ordination, take the rite to exorcise demons, as the Saviour had done when He had walked the earth.

As Fr Byrne stood at the foot of the bed he felt a sense of unreality: could such things be? One look at the sight before him revealed its awful truth. He donned surplice and stole, took from his pocket the bottle of Holy Water and sprinkled the bed. The figure in it recoiled in terror, telling him to depart as she belonged to them. He then blessed himself and began the ancient ritual of exorcism.

The sun had risen when Fr Byrne left the room and made his way down the wide stairway to where the young man was waiting. He asked him how long his lady had been like this, and what sort of devilish business had been going on in that place. He gestured to the young man that he would return that night and that he was to say nothing to a soul about this awful business. Having got an answer of sorts from the young man, who spoke little English, he decided to leave things for the present. And with that resolve he was driven back to his house.

Fr Byrne's heart sank as he sat that afternoon reading a book by the Jesuit Martin Del Rio, written in 1599, in which he listed no less than eighteen demonic apparitions. He also discovered, in another book, that the Church of his day, while preserving dogmatic belief in possession, rarely acknowledged the existence of possession in the modern world.

A few priests in Rome dedicated their lives to prayer and the study of diabolical possession, because theoretically they would have to pit their souls against Satan.

How could he have been so foolhardy? He felt unprepared for the task he had put on himself. There had been no time to consult his bishop, which meant that if he were to continue with the exorcism, he could find himself in trouble with his superiors. His courage almost failed him when he read that, in some cases, exorcism had lasted weeks, even months. The toll on his physical and mental resources would be immense, and he was a man well past his prime. His mind revolted against having to go to that room again that night, but a human soul was in peril. He would have to, no matter what the cost, continue, until she was released from the terrible bondage that held her captive. An hour later, he sent a message to the Jesuits in Dublin asking for their help.

The sun had set as Fr Byrne got into his horse and trap and prepared for the return visit. He had cautioned the young man never to speak of his visits to anybody. He considered it wise to travel after dark so as not to arouse suspicion, and hoped that their coach had not been seen coming to the presbytery the night before. He was all too aware of how difficult it was to keep a secret in a small village. As he commenced his journey, he thought of what to do next. Should he discuss it with the local vicar? What would be his reaction be if he told him of the true nature of his visits? When he arrived at Charleville House he gestured quietly to the young man who brought him up to the room and then departed. That night was to be a re-enactment of the previous one, only worse.

He donned surplice and stole, sprinkled the bed with Holy Water and began the prayers of exorcism. Never to his dying day, would he forget that night.

The sun had risen when the old lady finally fell into what he observed was a peaceful sleep. He was drenched in sweat, his mind numbed with horror. He was convinced that the power of prayer and the Sacred Host, which he carried on his person, had prevented him from being destroyed. The excerpt in his diary read:

Tuesday 6th June 1840

Exhausted and cannot continue without help. Have contacted Jesuits. Have had no time to come to terms with what I am confronted with and lament bitterly at the rashness of my conduct. Feel helpless but must continue. The Lord will not turn his face from his servant or go back on His word, which He spoke to the prophets of old.

He descended the stairs. His main concern was not to be seen coming or going. The gardeners hadn't arrived for work. He left the avenue and drove onto the main road. As he reached the village, the men were going to work in the fields. When he had said Mass, he went to bed.

The following afternoon, Fr Fennell, SJ, sat across from Fr Byrne in his presbytery as he unfolded the horror of the past two nights. Fennell was not uncompromising in his condemnation of Fr Byrne's rash conduct, nor did he need to point out the seriousness of the situation, not to mention its dangers. It was written on the priest's face. Fr Fennell, usually a loud cheerful man, spoke in a whisper. Fr Byrne, he said, would have to continue conducting the exorcism. Fr Fennell had a vast knowledge of demonology and continued to press him about every aspect of what he had witnessed. Having satisfied himself that the case had the hallmarks of demonic possession, he inquired about Pamela Ingram — who she was and the type of life she had led. The priest had little to tell him, only stories that were told around the parish. The rest of that day was spent in prayer and preparation for the night to come. As they made their way that night to Charleville House, Fr Byrne thanked God that He had sent Fr Fennell to assist him. That night would be a re-enactment of the previous two, only more violent. They were to spend another two nights in that room before their ordeal was to end. Fr Byrne was warned never to hold conversation with the demons, but to continue the exorcism come what might.

When they entered Charleville House, Fr Fennell sensed evil. As they ascended the stairs, he viewed the paintings lining the walls; the faces of generations of dead men and women stared out at him. He took a bottle of Holy Water from his inside pocket and began sprinkling it in front of him. When they reached the room, the young foreign man quietly opened the door then slipped away.

The room was large and decorated in a French style. The walls were covered with tapestries depicting the Four Seasons. It was a warm, still night and the windows were open. Over the mantelpiece was a large portrait of a young woman of indescribable beauty. It was the portrait of Pamela Ingram painted in her youth. Fr Byrne was now silently preparing himself. He had taken a bottle of Holy Water and put it on the dressing table next to the bed. Fr Fennell stood gazing at the portrait, unable to take his eyes off it. He scrutinised its every feature. The artist had captured the sitter's inner life. The eyes that looked out had an air of haughty defiance not noticed at first glance. Behind the flawless beauty an image emerged, cold and arrogant.

The bed on which the old lady lay was a four-poster, covered with a canopy. Fr Fennell silently walked over to it. The old woman was bald headed and sunken eyed, and at that moment her eyes opened. The look in them would remain with him for the rest of his life. He was filled with a mixture of pity and loathing, struggling to reconcile the creature on the bed with the painting that hung not a dozen feet away. At that moment, he felt an inconsolable pang of pity and terror at the loveliness and tragedy of all living things. The words of the Saviour rang out in his mind, 'if I be lifted up, I will draw all things to myself'. It was this that He had embraced on the cross. He was aware as never before of the mystery of good and evil. He took from his pocket his surplice and stole. Only minutes had passed since they had first entered the room, yet it seemed like an eternity.

Fr Byrne was standing silently, breviary in hand. Fr Fennell signalled to him and they made the sign of the cross and began to pray. The demons, speaking through the old lady, cursed and taunted them with violent death and final damnation, then pleaded with them, in the voices of children, to leave them in peace. They sang to them in voices so captivating that they almost faltered. Then they would boast of the many they had brought to perdition, of the many more that would be theirs. Fr Fennell stuffed Fr Byrne's ears with swabs of cotton wool so as not to be diverted by the awful taunts that were coming from the mouth of the old lady. He was alert, never allowing himself to deviate for a moment, observing. He was a man of courage, with nerves of steel. His order had for centuries been on the firing line whenever a human soul had been in peril. Their founder had taught that they must hold dialogue with the world, challenge the nature of good and evil, make judgements, and never back down in the face of the foe.

Daylight was streaming into the room when the figure on the bed finally fell into a sleep. Their night of struggle was over. They disrobed in silence. Fr Fennell walked over to the open window and gulped in the fresh morning air. Birds were singing in the Dargle Valley below, and in the distance, he could see Powerscourt House. He addressed Fr Byrne, 'We're done, Simon?' Fr Byrne nodded. They left the room with one last glance at the figure in the bed. Having closed the door, they made their way down to the hallway. The young servant arrived, it seemed out of nowhere. Fr Byrne spoke quietly with him. Fr Fennell observed that he spoke with a broken English accent. He was about to engage him in conversation but decided against it.

They drove down the long avenue, past the two marble lions that guarded the entrance to the house. Both men, though exhausted from the pervious night's ordeal, felt mentally alert, their minds still racing with unanswered questions. The road to the village was empty until they reached the entrance to Powerscourt House, where a coach-and-four pulled out to pass them.

Then they reached the presbytery, and over a cup of tea, Fr Fennell addressed Fr Byrne. 'Simon, I am taking over your parish duties until this business is over.' Fr Byrne was about to protest but was interrupted. 'You're in no condition to carry on without help.' Fr Byrne nodded his head in consent. It would have been pointless to argue with the man who sat opposite him. Apart from the beginnings of stubble on his face, there was little to indicate that he had spent the previous night confronting what they now believed to be a woman in the throes of demonic possession. After Fr Byrne had said Mass, he was ordered to bed.

After two hours rest on a couch in the presbytery, Fr Fennell said Mass, and then had breakfast. He went back to the church, where he knelt for hours before the Eucharist, after which he returned to the presbytery and went over the notes he had made the previous night. He was perturbed. He found the business too loose-ended and open to error. He knew that at the end of this ordeal, whatever the outcome, he would come in for criticism. The Jesuits laid down strict guidelines in these matters, culled from the hundreds of documented cases it had at its disposal. He knew his preparation had been slip-shod: he had not gone to Charleville House to see things for himself, to see the room and its occupant. He was angry that Fr Byrne had taken it on himself to carry out this exorcism without first consulting him. He had lost his objectivity in the matter, allowing emotionalism to guide him, which is anathema to the Jesuit mind. He was convinced that this was a case of demonic possession. Having witnessed the violence of the previous night, he considered that it could be a turning point, an indication that the demons were ready to depart but could also be a trick to lead them into complacency. His main concern was how long Fr Byrne could hold out.

Fr Byrne was up and about when he arrived back at the presbytery. He had taken a tour of the parish, stopping off to talk to people he had met. He addressed Fr Byrne, 'You're a blessed man Simon, to be living in such a beautiful place.' Fr Byrne related that his people had lived in the glens of Wicklow for generations. He spoke of his childhood, how he always wanted to be a priest, his studies in France. Fr Fennell liked this quiet-spoken man. He saw in him a dedicated priest who would do anything to protect his flock. He avoided talking about the business at hand. The rest of the afternoon he spent in reading and taking notes.

That night, as they made their way to Charleville House, they were silent, each lost in his own thoughts. Fr Fennell was focused on the night ahead; Fr Byrne gazed on the village he had served for so long. Two of his flock were on their way to the village pub. Most were indoors seeking their rest after the day's labour. At that moment he longed to be among them.

He was awakened from his reverie by the motion of the trap going over the bridge. When they reached the house, they were greeted by the young man, who brought them up to the room. When they entered all was silent. The old lady was sleeping. As they prepared to continue the exorcism, her eyes opened and they were to experience the malignant hatred that came from her. Fr Byrne began, in a calm voice, making the sign of the cross. Fr Fennell, ever the observer, wrote down every saying and gesture of the demons. He felt calm and in control, never once losing his sense of objectivity. The night wore on. Fr Fennell observed that Fr Byrne seemed stronger than on the previous night, his voice never once faltering. Somehow, he had found a new resolve. He moved closer to the bed, sprinkled it with Holy Water and commanded in a loud voice:

Be on to her, O Lord, a fortress of strength in the face of the enemy.
Let the enemy have no power over her.
And the son of evil does nothing to harm her.
Send her, O Lord, aid from on high.
And from Zion watch over her.
O Lord, hear my prayer and let my cry come onto thee.
The Lord be with you
And with thy spirit!

Hour after hour they continued. They lost all track of time. In that room time had ceased. Fr Byrne kept commanding the demons to depart and leave her in peace. Their curses, clamour and taunts told Fr Fennell that at last they might be ready to depart. With one mighty effort the two priests together commanded the demons, 'Go out from her! Depart to where you came from, in the name of the living God. In the name of the Word made flesh.'

The room was suddenly calm. The old lady looked at them with an indescribable look of peace. They knew at last the struggle was over. They fell to their knees and prayed silently. It was nearly 5a.m. The nightmare had ended. Fr Byrne put the crucifix in the old lady's hands. She sweetly kissed it.

It was the last time that the two priests were ever to take that journey. Fr Fennell returned to his order in Dublin, having compiled a full account of what he had witnessed. It would be scrutinised and put into the archives to be studied by future generations of Jesuits.

Fr Byrne's last entry in his diary read:

8 June 1840
Left C.H. at 5:30 having placed crucifix in hands of P.I. Have spoken with Fr Fennell on the true nature of what we had both experienced. Have no doubt that, without his help, all would have ended in failure, and worse. I thank God that the ordeal is at last over.
Simon Byrne PP

Pamela Ingram died at 10a.m. that morning.

Fr Byrne returned to his duties, his flock none the wiser of what their parish priest had been through, though many commented on his loss of weight. He did, in time, regain his health. Though somewhat withdrawn and introspective, he continued as their parish priest up until his death. He never spoke about his experience at Charleville House.

two

A Strange Happening

The evening of 7 September 1910, was for Matt Kinsella the same as any other. Matt lived with his widowed mother at Purcell's Field (off the Bray Main Street). He had come in from work about half past six, had his dinner, fed his birds and dogs, then dozed off while reading the paper. When he woke, it was twenty to ten and a wind had got up. He looked through the window at a watery moon, opened the back door and went to the shed. He took a handful of rabbit snares that hung from a nail in the corner. He then went over to a large cage that housed his ferrets. He selected one and put it in a sack. He re-entered the kitchen, put his coat on, and walked out into the night.

When he reached the Main Street he noticed two men were walking ahead of him. He stood in a doorway to avoid them and when they entered Cassell's pub (now Lenihan's), he moved on. As he passed the Town Hall, it was ten to ten. When he reached the bridge at Patchwork on the Killarney Road, he crossed over, making sure that nobody was behind him. He climbed the wall and dropped over into Oldcourt Glen. He passed the back of Glencourt House, noticing that the lights were lit in every room. The people who lived there were known for their musical evenings. He could hear the voice of a woman singing, and stood for a few moments listening, then moved on.

He knew every inch of this place and darkness held no fear for him. He had trapped it for rabbits since he was a boy, as had his father before him. Matt was in his prime, lean and tough from the long hours he spent in the fields working. He was a farm labourer, respected by all for the honest day's work he gave. His mother would boast proudly that farmers fought over her Matt. It had been a good year for saving the hay. The harvest had also been good. He had at various times worked for Smiths of Berryfield, Rialls of Old Connaught, Leesons of Ballyman, and once walked to Pat Whytes in Kilmacanogue to save the hay. Many farmers wanted him full time. He was considering getting married and settling down.

With a steady job and the money he earned from rabbits, he would do all right. He also bred terrier dogs and trapped wild birds, which was an added source of income. He was a thrifty man, not given to drink. He thought of his father as he silently made his way up the glen. He had taught him everything he knew. He would always repeat to him, 'If you can't do something on your own, get somebody you can really trust.' It was good advice that had stood him well. 'Pub talk is loose talk, remember that.' His father had been a hard man in his day. When Fr Mathew had come to Bray, he had taken the pledge for life and had never taken another drop till the day he died.

Matt felt a sense of wellbeing as he moved up the glen. He was blessed in his health and in his friends, Tom Boyd and John O'Brien. As he made his way up the bank and through the gap that led into the paddock next to Oldcourt, he stopped and listened. This was Lord Meath's land and strictly private. Technically, he had been breaking the law the moment he had put a foot in Oldcourt Glen, and men poaching rabbits could look forward to a stay in Mountjoy prison. They had been warned about a new gamekeeper recently employed by Lord Meath – a local man who knew all by sight.

He reached into his inside pocket to make sure he had not dropped any of the snares. The snares were for his two friends. As he did, the ferret in the bag started to move. The three of them were partners, dividing everything three ways. They would snare the surrounding fields that night after they had picked up the early catch. He skirted the field and made his way around to the path that led down to the summerhouse beside Oldcourt Lake. It was pitch black now. He had always found this part of Oldcourt eerie. He would never admit it to anybody, but the place filled him with an unknown fear. He consoled himself with the thought that his friends would be waiting in the summerhouse with a good mug of tea. He imagined he could taste it as he made his way through the darkness.

Tom Boyd, or Yip as he was known to his friends, was early as he made his way to the summerhouse in Oldcourt that night. The Dublin buyers had arrived at his house and he had got a good price for the rabbits without too much haggling. Tom was the eldest of the trio and had been selected to do all the selling. He had cautiously made his way down into Oldcourt from the Boghall Road, making sure to avoid the house, past the castle and on to the narrow path that led to the summerhouse. He gave a low whistle to see if his friends had arrived and, receiving no reply, he cautiously made his way to the side of the summerhouse. Seeing there was nobody there, he entered. It was warm; the embers of a fire were still evident. He took a kettle and filled it with water from a milk churn that stood in the opposite corner, put in on the fire, lit his pipe and waited for it to boil.

He reflected on the day that they had come up with the idea of using the summerhouse as a base for doing their business. It had worked well, as they now had enough money to go legitimate. They had been in touch with many of the farmers around the county. These contacts had come through his late father who was an exporter of rabbits to England. This meant buying the trapping rights to their land. He had also contacts in Liverpool. His father used to travel there with hundreds of boxes of rabbits for the English market. Tom intended to carry this on. The Dublin buyers were only giving them half of what they would get by dealing abroad. Rabbits were getting harder to poach around the local area. Lord Meath had employed the two gamekeepers to stamp out what he called the scourge of poaching. To be caught would mean going to prison.

Tom had selected his men well. Their fathers had been friends and had poached together for years. The plan had been a simple one: to save as much money as they could and travel the county buying the trapping rights from farmers. With their daily jobs, poaching at night remained a problem. To work for twelve hours a day, then to be out all night would tax the strength of even the strongest man. They also planned never to be seen together at night, as this would eventually arouse suspicion.

They then came up with an idea to meet at the summerhouse at Oldcourt. This was a circular building with three open archways into it, and it had seats and a fire grate. Lord Meath had built it when he bought Oldcourt in 1896. Its functions were varied: people could use it to shelter from the rain, it was a popular place for picnicking, swimming and boating on the lake, and the fishermen used it to hang their clothes if they got wet. It also housed the small punts that were used for boating on the lake. Tom and his mates had decided to use it as a place to rest during the night hours. The rabbits had to be collected before first light. Gamekeepers were the big danger, so they had to pick up any evidence that the area was being poached. The summerhouse was ideal, but there was only one drawback: local men would use it to congregate, drink and play cards. It was a chance they had to take. Everything was working to plan, and the money jingled reassuringly in his pocket. He was woken from his reverie by the hissing of the kettle. He took three mugs from his haversack, poured one, sat down, and waited. He hadn't heard Matt approaching, but when he looked around, he was standing and watching him. 'For Christ sake, man,' he growled, handing him a mug of tea, 'will you signal before you enter?'

John O'Brien was the youngest of the three, cheerful and easygoing, but dependable. He'd spoken of emigrating to England. Tom and Matt had discussed who would take his place in the event of his going. He felt light-hearted as he made his way to the summerhouse. Tonight he would get his share of the profit. He thought of the young woman he was taking out the following night. She was a country girl who worked as a domestic servant for Hodsons of Hollybrook. He walked across the paddock field, stopping once to listen when he thought he heard noises. He was carrying over a dozen rabbits. Their weight was starting to tell on him. He had taken up the snares and white pebbles, used to mark where the snare had been set, and could be seen in the dark. He made his way down the narrow path, gave a whistle, and having got the all clear he joined the other two. They sat and discussed the business at hand, having first shared out the money to the satisfaction of all.

What to do next was high on the agenda. Matt and the young John were in favour of carrying on as they were. Boyd argued that this could be foolish and dangerous. They had been lucky so far. He was all in favour of going legitimate. The argument got hot. Tempers were starting to rise. Matt and Tom argued about paying farmers when Lord Meath was supplying the rabbits for free. The Town Hall clock was striking when they decided to get a few hours' rest. 'We'll make a decision tomorrow when our heads are clearer', Boyd suggested. As they settled down to wait for dawn, something was to happen that would change their lives forever.

On the morning of 8 September 1910, Mrs Kinsella rose from her bed in Purcell's Field to begin another day. As she made her way to the kitchen, she could hear the sound of heavy footsteps as the men marched off to their work. She felt uneasy, as she had not heard Matt come in, and her worst fears were confirmed because Matt always lit the fire and would have a cup of tea waiting for her. Her first thought was that the police had caught him. Then all sorts of wild thoughts ran through her mind – maybe he was lying somewhere, having been shot by a gamekeeper, bleeding to death. How many times had she warned him about going out at night poaching rabbits? If he got jail what would she do? Matt was the only breadwinner in the house, her husband having died some years before. She went to the window and looked over to O'Brien's. She quietly walked over and knocked at the door. Jenny O'Brien let her in.

As the autumn sun stole into the kitchen, the two women sat silently, each lost in thought. Jenny O'Brien broke the silence, 'We'll have to do something.' Mrs Kinsella decided to go over to Leesons of Ballyman to see if Matt had gone straight to his work. If he hadn't, she would go to the barracks. They made a cup of tea and were ready to leave when there was a knock at the door. 'Thank God', said Mrs O'Brien as she rushed to open it. Mr Shortt, a neighbour, was standing there and by his side was her son, John. When she saw him, she let out a shriek. 'He's had an accident,' said Mr Shortt, 'I think you should call a doctor.'

Mrs Kinsella rushed to the door. 'Where's my Matt?' 'He's over in the house', replied Mr Shortt. Mrs Kinsella rushed into the house and huddled in the corner was her son. She stared at the human wreck before her. His face looked as if it had been kicked in with a pair of hobnailed boots. Anger welled inside of her. 'Who did this, Matt?' She asked. 'Was it the Polis? I'll tear their eyes out!' She could get no reply from him. 'I'll get the doctor.' Matt beckoned to her. She bent down and he whispered something to her.

An hour later, Dr Rafferty stood in the kitchen talking with her. He was a gruff man who never minced his words. The poor of Bray loved him. They saw in him someone who was on their side. 'Drink again. The curse of the nation,' he growled as he tended to young Matt. 'He doesn't touch it, Doctor,' replied Mrs Kinsella. 'Well, he didn't get this way picking his nose. He's been in a bad fight, and he's lucky to be alive. I'll give him something for the shock. I'll have the nurse up to dress his wounds.' After writing out a prescription, the doctor marched out of the house without another word. Mrs Kinsella had done what her son had asked, and soon after, Fr Gorman, parish priest to the Holy Redeemer, was standing in the kitchen. He went into Matt's bedroom, and when he returned, he seemed perturbed. 'Will he be all right, Father?' asked Mrs Kinsella. 'I mean he'll be all right? Won't he?' 'I've heard his confession and given him Holy Communion', the priest replied. 'There is nothing more I can do', and with that he left. When Mrs Kinsella looked out the window, she saw him walking over to O'Brien's. Rumours started to circulate about what had happened to Matt Kinsella and John O'Brien. They were to continue for a long time.

Matt Kinsella never recovered from that night and spent most of his time in his room. He would make an effort to go to work, only to run out of the field and home to his mother like a frightened child. The doctors could do nothing for him. He suffered from what they called fits of hysteria. Mrs Kinsella prayed day and night for him. 'What in the name of God happened to you, son?' she would whisper to him. All she ever got was a frightened stare from him. John O'Brien seemed to rally round, and left for England some time later. He never returned to Bray. There were rumours over the years. It was said that he had been killed in the war or that he had died in a mental asylum in England. The family never spoke of it, but it was known that he and Matt never spoke after that night. What of Tom Boyd? He seemed to have survived whatever had happened to them that night. He continued working, reared a family, and lived into old age, but maybe not without some consequences.

What really happened in that place, that night? Anyone connected with it or who knew anything about it, is long since dead. Oldcourt was hugely popular with tourists. People came from all over to boat and picnic there. It was also, according to local tradition, a place where locals would meet at night to play cards and drink. These sessions were said to have gone into the early hours. I remember hearing my mother mentioning them, but whether she heard my father talking or knew about them from another source, I cannot tell. (She was a Little Bray woman.) My father spoke of the Vevay men taking drink down from Doyle's shebeen, via a short cut that led through Fran Loughlin's field (now the soccer field behind Sugar Loaf Terrace). In the sixties, when we were digging holes to put down a chainlink fence that divides the property of Oldcourt, we

The Boathouse at Oldcourt, Bray, County Wicklow, c.2007.

unearthed stout bottles of that period, my father pointing out the route taken by the Vevay men down to Oldcourt.

There are two pieces of information that give the story a more sinister aspect. That grown men of that period could be reduced to gibbering wrecks after a fistfight, no matter how vicious, is hardly credible. Fistfighting was a way of life with them, and grudges after a fight were seldom held. The late Dan Pluck told me that eighty years ago in Bray such events were common practice. If a row did start in a pub on Saturday nights, the two men would go home and change their good suits so as not to have them torn, return, and then go behind the Town Hall to settle matters. They were tough breeds who were used to heavy manual labour. Men used to come from Dublin to fight local men for money. Bets would be taken on the winner. The late Sean Tobin told me how his grandfather Nutser fought one such man from the Liberties of Dublin in Dunne's yard in Little Bray. It lasted for over an hour. Some of these fights were so vicious that the shafts of a cart were used to separate them.

The physical wounds suffered by these men at Oldcourt that September night didn't heal, and are said to have resulted in a deformity of the features. The doctors who examined them could find no medical explanation. Fr Gorman suggested that the men go to Mount Argus to do a penance known as the 'Fifteen Saturdays'. The next piece of information we have is telling! My father told me many times that people used to gather at Bray railway station to catch a glimpse of the men who had been beaten by some evil entity.

When the lake in Oldcourt was cleaned in the early sixties, I worked on it with 'Gutty' McKenna and my father. Gutty had worked for years trapping rabbits (hence the nickname). One afternoon, working opposite the ruins of the summerhouse, we unearthed an old bucket of that period. He remarked that it could be the bucket used to carry plain porter on the night they were beaten up. He's the only other person ever to mention that event. I don't remember the rest of the conversation. Did he know any of the people mentioned in this story? He did tell me that years back he fished the lake at night. He found it a forbidding place. Did Gutty know any of them? Had he trapped rabbits with them? At the end of my father's life, he came up with more than the three names that were mentioned. He said that there were as many as six people involved. When he was a lad, my father would get sixpence on Saturday to take an old man via donkey and cart down to Bray to have him shaved. He was unable to do so for himself as his hands and body shook. He was the last surviving member of that group of men who were in the summerhouse on that September night. His name was Tom Boyd.

NOTES

I discovered in a book, *True Irish Ghost Stories* by St John D. Seymour and Harry L. Nelligan (third edition, 1926), of a case known in Drogheda which was very similar to what allegedly happened in the summerhouse at Oldcourt. It concerned a family who had rented a house, only to be subjected to a frightening ordeal culminating in two of their children and their nurse being badly beaten. The nurse died some days later. They were urged by their solicitor to sue for a refund of rent. Their case was brought before a Judge Kisby in 1895, who ruled in favour of the landlady, refusing to hear the testament of previous tenants, who had been subject to an experience of a similar nature.

It is alleged that an entity visited the men in the summerhouse at Oldcourt that night, after a fight had ensued and they had been badly beaten up. In the Drogheda case, the entity was a woman seen by the father and mother. The floorboards and furniture in the room were torn up, and a candlestick was hurled at the woman in the presence of her husband.

There was in Mount Argus, the Dublin centre of the Passionist Fathers, a Dutch priest by the name of Fr Charles, who was known for his ability to look into the souls of people. Was he there at the time these men are alleged to have gone for a cure? Is their case documented there? Was their story in the papers of the day?

My father was friendly with an old man named Jimmy Whiston. He might have got the story from him. Mr Whiston worked as a stonemason for Lord Meath, and did the repair work on Oldcourt Castle. His predecessor had been a land agent for the Edwards family.

The late Christy Brien, a local historian, is said to have known about this story. Forty years ago in Bray there might have been many old people who may have known this story. I would have never heard it if I hadn't worked with my father at Oldcourt.

three

A Traveller's Curse

As you cross Bray Bridge, there is a narrow road to the left that runs parallel with Bray golf course. It leads to Bray harbour on the right; to the left, on to the back strand. To the locals it has always been known as 'back sea road'. This stretch was used by generations of the travelling community as a halting site. Every summer their gaily coloured caravans could be seen parked, one behind the other, their horses grazing on the grass margin. The women drew water from the Dargle River to do their washing. The hedge was their washing line. Walking over the bridge you would see sheets and children's clothing fluttering in the wind.

These halting sites were long established by the travelling community. They would stay for short periods then move on, to Wexford and to other parts of the country, an endless cycle, repeated year after year, generation after generation. They were a people, close knit, with their own customs and language. The men were horse dealers and tinsmiths, mending pots and pans for the housewives of Little Bray. The women would go to the doors of the well-to-do, babes in arms, seeking alms.

Over the years, some became 'settled people'. Names like Cash and Moorhouse have long been connected with the Little Bray area. I remember old John Moorhouse who came to Bray from Wexford many years before. He was a butcher and horse dealer. His descendents still live in Bray. My mother told me that when there was a death in the

Footprint carved on parapet of Bray Bridge, Bray.

local community he would use a horse whip to round up his sons. Telling them, 'go to that decent man or woman's funeral'. Up to recent times, and for generations, all funerals went down Back Street, which was the heart of Little Bray. No matter how big or small the funeral, John and his sons would attend it.

Members of the travelling community have long been associated with Irish traditional music and song. John Reilly, ballad singer, and the pipers Johnny and Felix Doran are highly regarded in traditional circles. Every summer when Johnny Doran came to Bray, Tom O' Donnell, a fellow piper would take a week's holidays (he worked for the Railway Company) and they would pipe for a week at his campsite up at the

Silver Bridge (on the then main Wexford Road). Tragically, Johnny Doran was killed in Dublin in the fifties, when an old wall under which he was camped collapsed on his caravan.

Another less-known tragedy is associated with the Dorans. It happened many years before at the halting site in Bray. A young child playing on the banks of the river fell into the water and was drowned. His father was inconsolable. When the child's body was retrieved from the river he removed one of his shoes and walked up to Bray Bridge. With a chisel he hacked out the imprint of the shoe on the bridge, after which he is said to have put a curse on the river for having taken his child. Ever after that, when he passed through Bray he would go to the bridge and renew his curse. Any person walking over Bray Bridge who looks closely can still see the imprint of a child's shoe on the wall (sea side), and remember a curse, put there by his grieving father, on the river that had taken his child from him.

NOTES

This is one of the lesser-known tales of Bray. Up to recently, I was unaware of it. It was given to me by Peter Regan, and was given to him by Dick O'Carroll, who got it off an old resident of Little Bray. Those who labour in the field of folklore provide a valuable service in preserving that which otherwise might be lost forever. If the foregoing tale has anything to tell us, it is this: that the field is never gleaned; there is always another tale to tell.

four

Lover's Leap

The Dargle Valley is situated a few miles from Bray, County Wicklow. It is a place of great beauty, with the Dargle River running through it on its journey to the sea. It is dominated by a huge rock that juts out over one hundred feet above the valley. This rock is known as Lover's Leap and it has a tragic tale of doomed love and death attached to it.

Our story begins in the quaint little village of Enniskerry, a short distance from the Dargle Valley. It is the story of a boy and girl, very much in love. It was believed by all that they would marry. However, when a new family of some wealth came to live in that district, the eldest son started to woo the young girl with dash and charm. She became infatuated with him, and began to spend a lot of time in his company, much to the concern of the villagers who noticed that her first lover had become withdrawn. He was seen late at night walking alone in the Dargle Valley. He neglected his work, and was seldom seen in the village. Her new lover showered her with gifts and never allowed her out of his sight.

On a summer's day they were walking together through the Dargle Valley when they heard the village church bell tolling. It told of death. The young girl felt an icy hand clutch at her heart. She tore herself from her companion and frantically made her way to the village. When she got there, her first lover's coffin was being carried from the church. He

Lover's Leap, Dargle Valley, Enniskerry.

had died of a broken heart. Dazed with grief, she realised how much she loved him. Through her vanity she had been responsible for his death. At that moment she knew that her life was over, that she could not live without him. She went screaming through the village, pulling at her hair. The villagers looked, aghast, shaking their heads, as she disappeared across the fields.

News of her strange behaviour spread. She had been seen at dead of night making her way to the old graveyard where her young love was buried. She would then throw herself on his grave and lie there till the dawn had broken, only to repeat it the following night.

Sometimes she would run through the village in her nightgown. Then she would stop to tell people how she and her young love had walked through the valley at night, that they would soon be together, forever. The priest was sent for. He spoke to her. But nothing was to any avail. It was commonly believed that grief and remorse had unhinged her reason. It was suggested to her family that she be confined to the house, and that maybe in time the madness would go. The mother of the young man whose heart she had broken showed her no pity, nor did others in the village. They considered it a just penance for the way she had treated him. The young man who had wooed her disappeared from the picture. He had found new toys to play with.

It was the night before midsummer when the brother of the young girl went to her room only to discover that she had somehow escaped. He frantically made his way over the fields to the old churchyard. When he got to the gate he could see his young sister lying across the grave. When she saw him coming, she leaped up and made her way across the fields crying out, 'He is waiting for me!' Her brother frantically tore after her, but it seemed that she had taken wings. Her brother followed her into the Dargle Valley. She ran wildly shouting, 'I am coming, I am here.'

When she reached the rock that juts out over the valley, her brother was only feet behind her. But it was too late. With one last dash she reached the rock, crying, 'I am coming, my love', and she flung herself off the rock and into the valley below.

The following morning the villagers carried her mangled remains back to the village. Two days later, with little ceremony, she was buried in the north-facing part of the old graveyard, which was preserved for those who took their own lives. Her first lover lies in the same churchyard.

Legend has it, that every Midsummer's Eve a young white fawn is seen running through the Dargle Valley. It is said to be the spirit of this unfortunate young girl, doomed till the end of time to search for her lost love.

The story of the Dargle lovers has carried down to our own time. There are many young people in Enniskerry who have heard this story.

five

A Concealed Room

Stories of the Big House have always been part of Irish folklore. There are countless tales of haunting, murder and revenge associated with those places. These tales are to be found in every county in Ireland. Many believe it was a way that the peasant Irish had at getting back at those who had stolen their land, when the haughty landlord would get his comeuppance for closing a Mass path or desecrating a holy well, by visitations of the dead, sudden death, and whatever else a vengeful peasantry could level against them.

Powerscourt House, situated near the picturesque village of Enniskerry in County Wicklow, has an interesting story attached to it. It is the story of a room in the house that has remained blocked up for many years. In the early eighteenth century, the house had become so disturbed that Lord Powerscourt had sent for the parish priest in Enniskerry, who came and exorcised the entity, banishing it to a room, which was then blocked up. He had warned that the room was never to be reopened. As a reward, Lord Powerscourt gave him a plot of land on which to build a church.

About forty-five years ago I got to know Mrs Cox, who lived with her son Kevin in the back lodge of the Powerscourt estate, known as the 'Golden Gate'. One day, over a cup of tea, she told me that she had come to work in Powerscourt House as a young girl of sixteen. (She died in

Kevin Cox, Powerscourt Lodge, Enniskerry.

the late seventies aged ninety-six.) One of her duties was to dust the walls and ceilings. One of the older maids knew the story of the sealed room. One day she brought her up to it. There was nothing to suggest that there was a room there. The older maid demonstrated that there was, by putting her long duster through a small hole in the wall. (The bamboo cane was about thirty feet in length.) She also told me that if I went to the front of the house and looked closely I would see the room. It was the only one with curtains on it. I later did so, and sure enough, one of the windows had faded, wine-coloured curtains.

The late Ned Brady of Roundwood also knew the story of the room in Powerscourt House. He had got the story from his father, who, in his youth, had worked as a plumber for the firm of McCormack in the city of Dublin. In 1896, there had been a call from the Powerscourts that pipes were leaking, and were in need of urgent repair. He and some other men went out to Powerscourt. They were installed in the servants' quarters for the two weeks they were there. He related that, during that period, it was discovered that the trouble with the leaking pipes was coming from a blocked-up room in the upstairs of the house. The wall was broken down to gain access, and the job was completed. Ned's father told of a disturbance in the house after the room was opened.

In 1938, Lord Powerscourt married and he brought his new bride to live at Powerscourt. The late Kevin Cox knew Lady Powerscourt (Sheila Wingfield). He found her a kind and courteous person. It was he who told me that she had insisted that the blocked room was to be reopened and that in consequence of having done so she suffered psychological problems. Contrary to a recent programme on the life of Sheila Wingfield, in which it was stated that she loved Powerscourt House and was loath to leave it, Kevin told me the truth. Prior to her divorce, Sheila Wingfield spent some time in the Shelbourne Hotel. A doctor would attend her daily, giving her an injection of morphine.

Was Sheila Wingfield's flight from Powerscourt House the result of material unhappiness or the result of something more sinister, i.e. the opening of a sealed room and the warning of a priest given nearly 200 years before?

six

Shep

When Billy Cassells returned to his home in Bray one day in 1988, he brought with him a three-month-old collie pup which he named Shep. Shep was white in colour, with black markings. Billy had purchased him off a farmer friend in Ballymore Eustace. Shep was considered the best of the litter, and came from a long line of good working dogs. Billy lived in Garfield House on the Killarney Road. His farmyard was located behind the house. It was here that Shep began his working life. Billy was a wealthy man. He had two farms in Enniskerry, and grazing land in and around Bray. He also kept a milking herd of cows. Shep's young life was spent between Bray and Enniskerry.

His day began early, when he would round up the cows to be milked. In summer there were two milkings a day, which was a busy time of year for any dog. Life was good for him. He was doing what he was born to do. He had two 'squares' a day and a good bed to lie on in the haggard (barn). But things were changing. The world was changing, and so was Bray. Dairy farming was becoming a thing of the past, as was farming. Many of the old holdings had been sold for new housing development. Billy was getting old, and was not in good health. It was only a matter of time before Cassells's yard would be no more. During this grey period, Shep got to be old. There was very little to do anymore. His days were spent lying around the yard. He

Monica Brien with Shep.

had a companion in Crony Ryan, an old employee of Billy, who had taken to sleeping in the haggard.

One day in 1993, Billy went to a point-to-point. His great love was breeding and racing horses. He had been warned by his doctor never to drink again. Having returned with a good sup taken, he became unwell and was taken to the hospital, where he died some hours later. It was the beginning of the end. Some time later his sister died. The farmyard was sold for development, Crony was dead, and Shep was without a home. He had lived a sheltered existence, never venturing on his own further than the farmyard. Bewildered and lost, he began to hang about the Town Hall (at the top of Bray Main Street.) His predicament was noticed. Peter Regan would feed him and allow him to sleep on the floor in his shop. In time, Shep's survival skills kicked in. He attached himself to Andy Reilly and Monica Brien. Both lived in Kalimantan Park next to Cassells's yard. Monica adopted him, jealously guarding his every move. Every year she took him to Holy Redeemer church for the 'Blessing of the animals'. The general public became aware of Shep. One day, a well-intended lady took him home and gave him a bath. Monica heard of this and went ballistic. When she met the lady on the Main Street she physically assaulted her for interfering with her dog.

One Sunday morning in 1998, Andy Reilly was found dead in his home. Andy lived alone, so the neighbours rallied around, getting in touch with his family in England and making the house ready for their arrival. Andy had, over the years, worked for Billy Cassells. When Billy died he left him a few bob, and two wristwatches, one of which Andy gave to Peter Regan. Some time later, Andy had also given the second watch to Peter.

On the morning of Andy's funeral, as the church bell was tolling, Monica came running down to the church in tears to say that Shep had just died; which didn't come as a surprise. The vet had wanted to put him down, but Monica would not let him cross the door. After saying goodbye to Andy, things got back to normal. Monica was in deep mourning for Shep. It was later that Peter realised that the two watches which Andy had given him had stopped at the time the bell had tolled for his funeral Mass; which was exactly the time that Shep had passed away.

seven

Ghostly Bray and Environs

The following account was related to me by a Miss M__.

For years I have had a recurring dream. I am back in my aunt's home. I have gone upstairs to the room I once shared with my two sisters. I am looking for some item in a chest of drawers. Suddenly I am aware of a malignant presence entering the room. It is coming in through the ceiling above the door. I feel trapped. I cannot pass it to escape down the stairs. I try frantically to open the window, and then I wake up. This dream has never altered in the slightest degree. Paramount is the evil presence I feel, and the awful awareness that it intends to harm me.

It was some years before that that my aunt had this room blessed by a priest. She slept downstairs, under our room and claimed just before the dawn she was awakened by the sound of somebody walking across the room with the aid of a walking cane. She claimed it went on for some months before she spoke with a priest who came and blessed the room. After that, the tapping ceased.

We made some inquiries about the previous occupants and found that two sisters had lived there. One sister was an invalid and could only get about with the aid of a walking cane. In her latter years she was confined to that room, and died there.

There is nobody in the family to corroborate this story. It rests only on the testimony of my aunt.

The late Seán Troy once related an incident that had happened to him in a house in Connolly Square (off Bray Main Street). A couple, who were close friends of his, had recently married and had purchased a house there. On New Year's Eve 1972, he met them for a drink in Holland's Bar and they suggested that they all go back to the house and ring in the New Year. After they had done so, the woman of the house went to bed, leaving Seán and his friend to chat and drink. Seán related to me that he went to the bathroom, which was an outdoor toilet in the yard. When he was returning, his friend was also on his way there.

Seán sat and poured himself a drink, and then he became aware of three men sitting at a table staring at him. He noticed that the suits they were wearing were from the thirties. They were double breasted (Martin Henry's). One of the young men was redheaded. All, he noticed, had very pale complexions. He thought that while he had been at the bathroom they had called to the house, that they were friends of his hosts. His friend returned from the bathroom and they began chatting, totally ignoring the three men who continued sitting, staring at them. Neither made any reference to them. After another lapse of time Seán once more made his way to the bathroom. When he returned and sat down, he noticed that the three men were gone. He again presumed that while at the toilet they had up and left. He mentioned this to his friend who told him that he hadn't a clue what he was on about. Seán left and made his way home. He told me he felt very frightened at what had happened. When he arrived home he mentioned it to his father. His father knew about this house, and a similar experience that other people had seen.

Years later a man who lived at the same address was in hospital, dying. When friends and family came to visit him he complained about the three men who were forever standing at the foot of his bed. When asked to explain their appearance, he gave an identical description of the three men Seán Tobin claimed to have seen in the same house that this man had occupied for some years.

The following incident was related to me by a nurse. One morning in June 1965, when she was out in the back garden, hanging out some washing, she happened to look towards the house and she saw her uncle standing at the door. He was dressed in his Sunday best. She shouted at him to put on the kettle, she would be there shortly. When she got in to the kitchen he was nowhere to be seen. She thought it strange that he should have left so abruptly, also that he was all dressed up on a working day.

Some time later she was down at his house and asked him the reason why he had left so abruptly. He told her he had no idea what she was talking about. Later, he took her aside and asked her to explain what she meant. When she explained to him he became very quiet. Before she left that evening he took her to an adjoining room which contained a closet in the corner of the room; it contained his wedding suit. She explained to him that this was the suit she had seen him wearing a few days before. It was less than two weeks later that he died suddenly.

The first and only time I met and spoke with Mick Healy was in his house in Sallynoggin in the early seventies. I was a friend of his late son Paddy. We had been out walking on Dalkey Hill and he took me back to the house for a cup of tea. When we arrived, Paddy's mother made us something to eat. Soon after that, Mick arrived home. During the course of our conversation he asked me whether I knew a house on the Newtown Vevay named Rockbrae. I told him I did, and he went on to relate an experience he and his wife (who was present) had there, sometime in the late thirties.

He had been made an offer he couldn't refuse – a permanent, well-paying position, with cottage at Rockbrae. Mrs Healy told me they were over the moon at their good fortune, considering how hard it was to get any job in the thirties. They were near Bray Town and the schools were only minutes away. It was a happy couple who made their way out to Bray to begin a new life. Mick told me that the job suited him; he

Rockbrae Cottage, Newtown Vevay, Bray.

was good with horses, and these people kept and trained horses, which would be his job. Mrs Healy then told me that things went well, but there was a strange oppressive feeling about the place. She felt she was being watched; she began to hear noises. She went into the room where she had heard the noise only to find everything to be in order. The noises became more numerous, and more violent. She was becoming very frightened, but decided to say nothing to her husband. Then he began to hear them. Both of them would lie awake listening to the dreadful racket going on in the kitchen; pots, and pans being hurled against the wall. When they went out to investigate, the noise would stop and everything would be in perfect order. This would go on all night. They told me they couldn't get to sleep. They both became terrified. When Mick went to work, Mrs Healy told me she would stay out of the house most of the day, afraid to go back there until Mick came home from work.

After only two weeks there they were both nervous wrecks. Their youngest child couldn't sleep and cried incessantly. Something had to be done. They spoke about the consequences of leaving. What would their employer, or indeed their families say when they told them the reason for leaving a steady job? Because a ghost was running around their kitchen, banging pots and pans off the walls? They decided to stick it out, and maybe things would level out.

They didn't; after only twenty-eight days they fled the cottage. Listening to their story I have no reason to doubt it. Paddy later told me it was the first time he had ever heard his father talk about it. He also said that as a young child he suffered from bouts of hysteria. He would be sitting in his classroom then suddenly he would jump up from his seat and run home to his mother. Could this have been a result of the terror he had felt as a baby in Rockbrae cottage?

In 1958, there was a force eleven storm which caused havoc around the country. The lighthouse in Bray harbour was blown into the sea. Up at Oldcourt, a very ancient beech tree was split down the centre by a bolt of lightning. The following day the Colonel sent for me and told me I could have the tree for firewood. (We were taking timber off that tree for over a year.) It was soon after that he told us a story that happened the night the tree had come down. He was woken by the crash of the tree falling, and the barking of his dog. When he walked out to investigate, the dog ran ahead of him to the gateway that led onto the main pathway. When he reached the gate, the dog was standing looking onto the pathway, whimpering. He opened the gate and began to walk towards the paddock where the tree stood. He then became aware of a person walking up and down the avenue, looking in to the paddock where the tree had come down. He told us he had never seen a taller person in his life. He stood for some minutes watching this person walking up and down the avenue. His dog stood behind him, whimpering, not daring to go further, which was totally out of character for him. He turned and went back into the house, not daring to approach the figure on the pathway. He said that the behaviour of his dog had really spooked him.

During the twenties the groundsman in Oldcourt was a man called Barrington. He was an employee of Lord Meath, who still owned the property. He lived in Rose Cottage on the Boghall Road. My late father knew this man. He was exceptionally tall, standing over seven feet. He died in the early thirties.

In 1989, my wife, daughter and I were passing Christ Church in Bray. The door of the church was open. My daughter expressed a desire to go in and have a look. We entered the church. There was a lady arranging flowers and vegetables (it was the harvest thanksgiving). We asked her would it be okay if we looked about. She said she would be delighted. After we had looked about, we prepared to leave. On the way, we thanked her, and then stood chatting about the church in general. She then told us of a strange incident that had happened to her as she sat in the congregation one Sunday morning some years before. She went on to relate that her husband had died suddenly, leaving her with young children. After the shock and grief of losing him, she got down to the business of bringing up her young family. It was a full-time job, which left little time for social activities. Time passed, and one night at a function she met a man who she was instantly attracted to. She never thought she could ever love another man. She was so riddled with guilt that she went to see her local vicar. She told him all. He was sympathetic, but firm. He told her it was time to move on with her life, that her husband would want her to. She married him. Later she realised how wise her vicar had been. She was happy, though she often thought of the father of her children. They, in time, were crowded out with her new-found happiness and the new demands that new beginnings bring.

She played an active role in her church, and was a faithful attender at Sunday service. On that particular Sunday morning, the church was unusually packed. She had returned to her seat having received

Communion. As she sat, watching the rest of the communicants returning to their seats, she froze. Walking down the centre aisle was the figure of her dead husband. My wife, daughter and I looked at her in amazement. Here was a young, poised, attractive woman telling us with complete matter-of-factness the story of having seen her dead husband. When we got outside the church, I remember remarking to my wife and daughter that it was the guilt she still felt of having married another man that had made her see her dead husband. My wife and daughter were not so sure.

☀ ☀ ☀

The following story was told to me twenty years ago by a young man I met and was never to meet again. He would have been about twenty-six years old. He was definitely not the type I would have expected to tell the story he did. He related to me that one night, some years before, he was a passenger in the car his father was driving. They were on a stretch of road that leads out at the Windgates to the Bray Road. They were passing the entrance that leads into the ruin of Belmont House on Lord Meath's property, when a woman walked out in front of the car. His father braked so violently that the car went skidding all over the place, ending up in the far ditch. They both got out of the car, badly shaken. They then began to look under the car, believing they had dragged the woman with them. To their surprise they couldn't see anything. Thinking that maybe the impact had hurled her into the ditch, his father went to the car for a flash lamp and they began searching. To their growing amazement they couldn't find a trace of the woman. They again reasoned that the impact had been so great as to hurl her into the field. They searched and searched but still no dead or injured woman could be found. Having searched for almost an hour, they decided to drive home and await further developments. Their first reaction was to call the police, but what would they tell them? They decided to wait till the following day and see would there be news of the accident on the radio.

The first thing they did the following morning was to examine the car for dent marks. To their growing bewilderment, there were none.

They decided to drive back to where the accident had occurred. When they arrived they had no difficulty locating the skid marks on the road. They resumed their search, convinced that they would eventually find the remains of the woman. They searched every inch of the road and the ditches on both sides, but to no avail. They drove home, totally bewildered by the whole event. For days they listened to the radio and TV for news of the accident but none ever came. It was after some length of time that they finally had to admit that what happened to them that night had no reasonable explanation to account for it. They were both shaken by what had happened. His father could never accept anything other than a rational explanation for what had happened to them. To the time of his son telling me, he still hadn't come up with one.

***

Some years back I was hitching a lift on the Roundwood road when I was picked up by a woman driving a jeep. When we got to Calary she told me of an incident that had happened to her some time before. She was travelling the same stretch of road. When she was passing Calary bog, the vaporised form of a woman floated across the window of her car. In her panic to avoid what she believed was a person, she almost crashed her car. She said it had happened in daytime and was in no doubt about what she had seen.

Some years before, a friend of mine and his wife had the same experience at the same place. Their experience was exactly the same as experienced by the woman driving the jeep, except that the event happened to them at night.

***

A friend of mine told me of an experience he had in the village of Rathdrum in County Wicklow. He and some friends went to the local pub to listen to music. After the session he went back to a friend's house in the village to stay over for the night. He related to me that as he was lying in bed, the scene in the room changed. What he saw enacted was a scene which he later described as a massacre. Women and children were being pursued by redcoats. There was screaming, children being bayoneted, mothers trying to protect them. He doesn't know how long this lasted. He told me the fright he got was so severe that he couldn't get to a bathroom in time, an accident that caused him never to be asked there again!

Later, he described the incident to a man who had a considerable knowledge of military uniforms. After describing the dress of the soldiers, what the woman and children were wearing, and also the type of weapons used, he was told that what he had described was the costume worn in 1798. The people's clothing also reflected that period. I questioned him again. I have no doubt that what he told me is true.

NOTES

A Protestant vicar had many years before hung himself in the cottage. A family named Carroll lived there for many years. I have never heard any other account of any disturbance connected with that place.

Back in the fifties, Colonel O'Kelly leased Oldcourt House. My father worked on and off for him. I spent a lot of time at Oldcourt and got to know the Colonel quite well. He was a career soldier who had fought in the Great War. He was awarded the DSO, having barely survived after being badly wounded. He was a remarkably fit man for his years. He had single-handedly cut away over fifty years of ivy from the castle walls at Oldcourt, lowering himself over the top with the aid of a pulley and rope. He said little, but got on with the job of cleaning up Oldcourt after years of neglect.

I would hope that this now middle-aged man might read this story and make contact after all these years. It would be interesting to see what his views are today.

After tracing his family tree, he discovered that an ancestor was a soldier in the Cork Militia and was stationed in that vicinity during the 1798 Rebellion.

eight

Was St Kevin a Murderer?

One of the most enduring legends of County Wicklow is the story of Kevin of Glendalough, and the woman, Kathleen, who fell in love with him. There are two versions of the legend. The first is that Kathleen had fallen madly in love with the young monk. He was to know no peace; she followed him everywhere, begging him to return the love she had for him. One day she followed him into a wood where she attempted to seduce him. Kevin, in a fit of rage, flung Kathleen into a clump of nettles. The pain brought her to her senses. Kevin sat her down and began talking with her. After he had finished she repented. She threw herself at his feet, begging his forgiveness. She is said to have become one of his most ardent converts, dying a saintly death many years later at Glendalough.

The other version of the legend has a more violent and tragic ending. A young and beautiful girl named Kathleen, who lived in the district of Glendalough, had fallen madly in love with the young monk Kevin. She pursued him relentlessly, imploring him to return her love. One night, in desperation, she made her way to his cell, which was situated hundreds of feet above the lake in Glendalough. She waited for him to return. When Kevin returned to find her in his very cell he is said to have fallen into such a rage that he flung the young woman into the lake below, where she drowned. If this legend is true, it makes Kevin of Glendalough a murderer.

The early fathers of the Church had a deep distrust and hatred of women. Down through the ages misogyny has run deep within the Catholic Church. The reasons are many and varied. The early fathers looked to the scriptures to validate this distrust. It was woman who had tempted man. It was through her that sin and death had entered the world. Another absurd reason for this wholesale hatred was that during the menstrual cycle, women were said to go temporarily insane and were not capable of making weighty decisions. Paramount was the idea that woman, the temptress, could through her wiles tempt man into sin, thus putting his very salvation in peril.

These thoughts would have been uppermost in the mind of Kevin. He would have seen in Kathleen the very embodiment of evil, come to tempt him away from what God, in a vision, had shown him – to establish a monastery in Glendalough that would in time become the glory of the Christian world.

It's not hard to imagine the scene that took place in that lonely cell 1,400 years ago when Kevin returned to find Kathleen waiting for him. When he recovers from the shock he implores her to leave him in peace. He feels in great peril. Kathleen will not be dissuaded. She moves towards him, begging him to make love to her. With one last resolve he pushes her violently towards the mouth of the cave, sending her hurtling to her death below.

We can only speculate what might have happened after that. Did Kevin climb down to the lake and raise the alarm? Was the body of Kathleen ever recovered? Was there ever an inquiry into her death? Did Kevin lie to save his own skin? Did Kevin deliberately throw this hapless girl to her death, whose only crime had been to fall in love with a saint?

Kathleen's spirit is said to haunt the ruins of Glendalough till the end of time. Many songs and ballads have been written about her. The following was sung by no less a personage than the writer Brendan Behan, who got the song from a man in the Wicklow glens:

In Glendalough there lived a young monk,
Who spent his days in austerity,

His manners were curious and quaint,
He looked on girls with disparity.

He was fond of reading a book,
When he get one to his wishes,
He was fond of casting his hook,
In among the young fishes.

One day he landed a trout,
He landed a fine fat trout, sir,
Kathleen, from over the way,
Came to see what the young monk was about, sir.

Keep out of my way said the monk,
I am a man of great piety,
My good manners I wouldn't taint,
With mixing with female society.

Kathleen wouldn't give in,
And when he came home to his rockery,
He found her seated within,
Polishing up his crockery.

He gave the poor crater a shove,
I wish a copper had caught him.
He flung her into the lake,
By Heavens she sunk to the bottom.

The following quotations from the *Latin Life of Saint Kevin* by Dr O'Donovan is apt to cause apoplexy within the ranks of the feminist movement. He quotes:

As a gross calumny had been committed to the durability of type and rendered celebrated by the verse of the last bard and historian of Ireland

(Moore), it devolves upon us as a duty to vindicate the saint's character from so foul an imputation as that of murdering a lady who was in love with him. The saint had no wish to kill the girl.

When he was growing up in the first flower of his youth, a young girl saw him in the field along with the brethren, and fell passionately in love with him. He was exceedingly beautiful. She began to make known her friendship, by looks, by language and sometimes by messenger, but the holy youth rejected all these allurements. On a certain day, she sought the opportunity of finding him alone. She approached him and clasped him in her arms in fond embrace. But the young soldier of Christ, arming himself with the sacred sign made strong resistance against her. He rushed out of her arms into a wood, the girl pursued him, he took a bunch of nettles and struck her on the face, arms and feet, and when she was blistered by the nettles and sorrowful at heart, she asked on her bended knees, pardon of Kevin in the name of the Lord, and the saint, praying for her to Christ, she promised him that she would dedicate her virginity to the Lord. The Brothers finding them thus discoursing together wondered, but the virgin related to them what had passed. That girl afterwards became a prudent and holy virgin and a diligent observer of the admonishments of Kevin.

On 2 November 1974 (All Souls' Day), a party of American tourists arrived at Glendalough. Among them were Mrs Everette Chisamore and her daughter Doreen. Glendalough was their last port of call on an itinerary that had taken them to Venice, Paris and London. It was a bitterly cold day, and they hurried through the ruins of Glendalough to keep warm. Having looked about, Mrs Chisamore and her daughter decided to return to the bus and wait in its comfort for the rest of the party to return. On the way out, they decided to take one last photo of the famous round tower. Having done so, they returned to the bus. Little did they know that this photo was to have international reverberations.

Some weeks later, having returned home to Watertown, on the Canadian border, they and some friends were going through the photos, when one of them asked who the lady in red walking on the pathway

Ghostly figure at Glendalough.

towards the round tower was. Sure enough, there was the figure of a woman dressed in what looked like clothes out of another age. The women were amazed. They swore that nobody was on the pathway when they took the photo, and that none of the women in their party was wearing skirts. They were totally bemused. They decided to print their story, with a copy of the photo, in a local paper. They were unprepared for the number of phone calls they received.

Among the phone calls received was one from a Mr Holzer, who assured them that such phenomena are not unusual, and that he had worked with mediums who had used psychic photography to a remarkable degree. The film used in Glendalough was a size 110 Kodak, colour, purchased in Amsterdam. Another phone call they received was from a Mr Fuller from Maryland. He claimed to have seen a woman in Glendalough who was identical to the one in the photo.

They decided to write to the 'Mayor of Glendalough' to see if he could shed any light on the matter. At this stage of their inquiry they knew nothing of the legend of Kathleen. They received a reply from Glendalough. They were told that five years earlier, to the day, carpenter Leslie Armstrong and his fiancée Emily Brown were walking in Glendalough. Emily took a photo of her fiancé. When it was developed it showed the figure of a woman standing beside him. It was identical to the photo that Mrs Chisamore had taken.

The figure is wearing eighteenth-century clothing. Kathleen lived in the sixth century. The mystery still remains. Who is the figure in the photo? Is it real? Or just an elaborate hoax? Those experts who have examined the photos swear to their genuineness.

NOTES

'St Kevin's Cell' is situated hundreds of feet above Glendalough lakes.

Bill Fanning, 'The Shepherd of Glendalough', told me that in the twenties he rowed G.K. Chesterton and George Bernard Shaw, 'two book writers from England', over to St Kevin's Bed. He also told of a young English woman of that period who had seen the figure of a lady in red, walking among the graves at Glendalough.

nine

The Vault

Mervyn Edward, 7th Viscount Powerscourt, inherited the title from his father in 1844, when he was just eight years old. His mother took charge of the affairs of the estate until he came of age in 1857. She had remarried and was then known as the Marchioness of Londonderry. As she relinquished her responsibilities in the estate, and to mark the occasion of her son's twenty-first birthday, she offered the parish the parting gift of a new church. Its position was more convenient for those parishioners who lived in the village and had the added advantage of preserving his Lordship's privacy. The old church at Powerscourt House had a thriving congregation and the rapid expansion of the neighbourhood meant that more people could be expected, all of whom would have to use the main drive to reach the church for services and, not least, tie their horses to his trees.

It is at this point that our story begins. To those acquainted with the old cemetery at Powerscourt, they will be aware that it contains burial vaults. The nearest one is next to the avenue. As stated, during divine service the horses were tied to the railings and trees. Many of the parishioners were aware that many of the horses became frantic with fear when they were tethered at the railing next to the vault. Rumours started to circulate about what might be the cause of such commotion. The Protestant community are a people not given to superstition, so little was spoken of the matter. Not long after these events they moved to their new parish church and the matter was quickly forgotten.

But truth has a way of resurrecting itself, and what was later to emerge proved both bizarre and frightening.

Old John Carroll lived at the back lodge on the Powerscourt estate. Every night he walked the three miles to the village of Enniskerry for his pint and the three miles back. He told the story of hearing strange noises coming from the vault next to the main avenue, a story that was received with some scepticism. It was commonly held that the reason he told that story was that he was afraid that some rogue might follow him some night and rob him.

The same couldn't be said about little Millie Dawson, who swore on a stack of bibles that she too had heard a strange noise like an explosion coming from the same vault.

Many of the old folk still remembered the story of Pamela Ingram and warned their children never to go near that place. It must be remembered that up to recent times Catholics (under pain of mortal sin) were not permitted to enter a Protestant church, not alone a cemetery. And so this story entered into the bloodstream of the village like so many across the length and breadth of Ireland, to be told around the fireside on winter nights of how the rich and mighty had got their just reward for the persecution they had inflicted on the peasant Irish, only in this case fact proved stranger than anything even the most vivid imagination could conjure up.

The next we hear about this alleged occurrence is in Paris. In the nineteenth century it was the custom of the rich to take what was known as the Grand Tour, a finishing school for wealthy young men and women. The person in question was a Miss M. whose brother had written an account of an inquiry which had been conducted into the aforementioned. Miss M. and her brother both lived in the vicinity of Powerscourt and she outlined the facts leading up to the inquiry.

It had come to the notice of the vicar and other leading members of the parish (all people of the highest integrity) that something indeed was amiss and they had decided to conduct a private inquiry into what was either mischief or something of a more unexplained nature. Among those selected to conduct it was the Bishop, also a physician and some important people in the vicinity.

On opening the subterranean chamber, the coffins were found in great disorder, not only scattered but lying in some cases one upon the other. Only three were undisturbed, one of a very old devout lady, and the other two of young children. It was thought desirable to appoint a commission. The coffins were replaced in proper order and the pavement taken up to make certain that that there was no subterranean means of ingress. The floor and steps were covered with fine ashes, a guard of soldiers set which kept watch during the night as well as the daytime, and at the end of three days the vault was again opened. According to the writer of the only available documented account, the conditions of things were worse than ever before. Not only was every coffin, with the same three exceptions, displaced, and the whole collection scattered in confusion, but many of them, weighty as they were, had been set on end, so that the head of the corpse was downward. Nor was this even all. The lid of one coffin had been partially forced open, and there projected the shrivelled right hand of the corpse it contained, showing beyond the elbow.

No trace of any footprint was to be discerned upon the ashes spread for the purpose of detecting intruders, and nothing in or about the coffins had been carried away. On the other hand, subsequent inquiry showed that the dead man whose arm was thrust out had died by his own hand. The matter had been hushed up at the time through the influence of the family, and the self-destroyer had been buried with the usual ceremonies, but the fact transpired and was known by many, that he was found with his throat cut and the bloody razor still grasped in his bloody right hand.

A Mr O. declares that he too heard this account in Paris from the lips of Mlle von G., whose father had conducted a similar inquiry. It is not

The Old Powerscourt Cemetery, Enniskerry.

stated where this event occurred. The facts were subsequently confirmed to him by her brother.

In the Irish case the family took the decisive step of burying the coffins separately, after which no further trouble was experienced. We are also told that the commission drew up a formal report of the proceedings which was lodged, but in 1899, when Count Perovsky-Petrovy-Solovovo, a well-known member of the English Society for Psychical Research, wrote to make inquiries, it was alleged that no such document could be found. At a later date, the Count did obtain from a member of the family a definite assurance that the sensational episode of the coffins was still remembered and that many professed to know that an official report had been drawn up. Such phenomena are not uncommon. For the past 1,000 years there have been documented cases of a similar nature in every country in all ages.

If the reader will permit me, I will digress for a moment to cite among many a case similar to the one we have discussed, to prove that what happened at Powerscourt was by no means an isolated case.

At Staunton, in Suffolk, is a vault belonging to the family of Frenches. On opening it some years ago, several leaden coffins with wooden cases, that had been fixed on biers, were found displaced, to the great astonishment of most inhabitants of the village. It was afterwards closed, and the coffins again placed as before; when about seven years ago, upon another member of the family dying, they were found a second time displaced, and two years after, they were not only found off their biers, but one coffin, as heavy as to require eight men to raise it, was found on the fourth step leading to the vault. Whence arose this operation, in which, it is certain, no one had a hand?

Such cases have been investigated by people of the utmost integrity. In dealing with such phenomena common sense must be our guiding principle. For every true happening, no matter how unexplainable, there are countless frauds. People who investigate such phenomena have nothing to gain. Doctors have more to do with their time than to spread ashes on the steps of burial vaults. All in question have more to do with the living than with the dead.

Almost forty years ago, my late friend Sean Messitt and I found ourselves in the old cemetery in Powerscourt. It was a beautiful August afternoon. We were standing at the wall about six paces from the vault of one Capt. Needham when I heard a horrific noise coming from the tomb. Remarkably I said nothing to my friend. It was only when we were on our way home that he turned to me and asked had I heard the noise which had come from the vault. Later, I thought about this incident and came to the conclusion that it was a device which used to be used in corn fields to frighten off crows. To those unacquainted with this device, it resembles the firing of a cannon. I decided to investigate. I walked the fields for a radius of about two miles surrounding the estate but there was not a corn field in sight.

NOTES

In past ages, people who took their own lives could not be buried in consecrated ground, regardless of their prestige. Hence the cover-up by the family concerned.

ten

Letters to a Priest

This well-attested account, as the title suggests, comprises letters to a priest. The events occurred in 1928 in County Wicklow. The name of the person (the woman of the house) and the name of the place are not disclosed.

The priest in question lived in England and the letters came to him by way of a fellow priest in County Wicklow who had a first-hand account of the very weird happenings that occurred at this woman's home over a period of six weeks. At this point it might be advantageous to read what the recipient of these letters had to say regarding the character and disposition of the woman and other members of this hapless family:

In connection with these accounts I venture to submit, for what it is worth, the evidence of this peculiar case. It is a specimen of a type of disturbance which is by no means rare, but which owing to such causes of shyness or fear of ridicule, illiteracy on the part of the sufferers, rarely attracts public attention. Some time ago Father M.N., a priest in Ireland, and member of a Religious Order, was kind enough to bring this alleged manifestation to my notice, and with the writer's permission to send on the letters he had received upon the subject. One gathers that the writer of the letters is the wife of a decent farmer in a somewhat remote district in County Wicklow. Obviously, as the letters show, there is no thought of self-advertisement, or wish to attract publicity; no familiarity with poltergeist literature. It also seems hard to understand how some of the incidents described could have been the work of some mischievous child. We give the letters in the order they were received by the priest who sent them to me.

M. L., County Wicklow
5th Nov 1928 Father M.N.
A very extraordinary happening has occurred in my house and place for the past six weeks and is still going on. I cannot account for it, unless it is what people call a 'Pishogue' or a demon sent to annoy us. The inanimate things move within the house, the bedclothes are taken off the bed and go out at the window. Any article taken goes as far as the boundary of my land and is found. I have three children, 14, 12, and 10 years. The eldest (a boy) sees nothing. The two younger (a boy and girl) say they see strange people about the farm and sometimes at the window. There are people about the farm and sometimes at the window. There is a tapping at the window heard very often, and scraps of paper found around with threats written on them. We were annoyed while saying the Rosary on Saturday night. We got pinches in the head and balls made of paper thrown as if from the ceiling. These things are recurring all the time. I had our own C.C. [country curate], Father D. say Mass in the house three weeks ago, but still the thing goes on. I have great faith in the Holy Mass to conquer this thing, whatever it may be. Mrs J.O. is my sister-in law and was here yesterday. She advised me to write to you.

The letter is signed in full and ends with a request to the priest to offer Mass for the cessation of the trouble, an alms being enclosed. The next letter, dated 12 November runs as follows:

Very many thanks for your kind and sympathetic letter. I shall do all those things you mention. I have given small phials of Holy Water to the children and grandmother who lives with us. It still goes on. Yesterday it was very active, the knives, clothes, pieces of soap thrown around the house. Grandmother's cap was pulled off while we were at the cows, and she is much annoyed as she is almost eighty years. About the same time my two younger children were out in the front field where there are some stacks of straw. An old woman took the overall she [presumably the little girl] had on and told her she would take her dress off if she were around again, as she wanted it for her own. The little brother was with her. They tell me there were a great many around the straw; they thought only a few men with flowing grey beards wearing high hats. The most were women and small boys barefooted; they thought some dressed in white. All had leather belts round their waists. One seemed to be walking on his head; they thought he had no feet. I now keep them inside as much as I can. The overall was on the gate next morning. It had an Agnus Dei in the pocket and it was not touched. Very little of the straw was found burned.

I had a servant maid since January until this thing commenced in September, when she was reprimanded about some meat found outside on the field; she left that evening. The servant boy tells how she was up at nights previous to that, he heard her laughing and crying at intervals. The threats came in scraps of paper and signed with this girl's name (K. O'N.). In one 'We will work it on you while the three of you are there.' 'It is a pity I cannot work it harder.' 'I will come down the chimney tonight and take Nana's glasses', and several other threats saying, 'It is over now, it is on for five weeks.'

On Saturday last I took my three children to confession. Our C.C., Father D. would not give absolution to my eldest boy, as he would not admit he was doing these pranks. I am quite positive that this thing is a charm or something worked by the girl I had. I shall take the child to another priest, on Saturday, and before he hears his confession I will explain what Father D. did. Will you offer Holy Mass that this thing may come to an end?

A third letter was written a week later (23 November). It runs as follows:

Very many thanks for your letter. The trouble still continues, but not as active as it was. The written scraps of paper are still coming. It was only yesterday we were forced to take any money we had in the house to the bank, as it was written on one of the scraps of paper we would be left without a penny. There were some few shillings taken, and I got written slips saying it was they took it. I also had my younger boy home from school and was told if I did not take him along he would be well pulled while I was away. He got several pinches that morning. One Saturday evening about 4 o'clock, my little daughter, aged ten and a half years, said she saw the servant maid I had employed ride up the yard on a horse, her mother following after on a motor bicycle, and then followed a long train of red-coated figures on horseback. The servant said, when passing the child, 'Good-bye, May, for ever.' In the slips of paper found in the house it was written that they were going to C., that is a farmer residing about half a mile away, but within the parish. I have heard that these occurrences have started there now. Some of the slips of paper are signed, 'K. O'N.' That was my servant maid's name. They seem to hear every word that is spoken in the house, because answers are written on some of the slips. I do anything you desire me; my relatives have joined me in the Novena to St Gerald.

The last letter (which is in the same handwriting as the first two) runs thus:

19th Jan. 1929
Revd and very dear Father M.N.
Many thanks for your letter of the 5th which I duly received. You can send my letters to Father T., and should he want any further details I shall let you have them as well as I can. The trouble now seems to have disappeared; we have seen nothing for more than a fortnight. The last thing we had was a queer looking black cat. It would seem very small at times and very big at other times with very long hind legs. It would get into a bed during the day and give annoyance. In the evening the younger children could see it get out of the window, though it was shut. It would get into a hen coop sometimes as if killing a rat, but in

reality the eggs were taken. Some time before this cat appeared, we did away with our own two cats. There was also a pickaxe taken from us and returned broken with the broken pieces also, saying how it was used at the other house and they could not help breaking it, that was in one of the old scraps of paper.

My husband was coming from the farmyard after looking up the cattle before going to bed, and when coming near the house, he would hear a great many voices, as if there were a number of people in the yard. Although he was nervous to come on, as he was alone, but when he arrived at the house he saw nobody, but he did not go alone after that, as he was afraid. That was also when the trouble was coming to an end. I shall never forget your kindness to me and my family, etc. M.K.

Extravagant and preposterous as much of this must seem, there are curious features of interest in it. If the first letter stood alone, one would be inclined to say that it conformed in many respects to a type of poltergeist story which is quite well attested.

The pulling off of the bedclothes is one of the commonest features (witness the Enniscorthy case recorded by Sir William Barrett) and so also is the movement of inanimate objects. When the writer says, 'We got pinches in the head', she seems to include herself, and one wonders if a child could play such a prank upon the mother without detection. Fr D. obviously believed that the elder boy was the culprit, and he probably knew the family well.

On the other hand, it is possible that in such cases, when some strange excitement, such as unaccountable movements, knockings and whisking off of bedclothes, comes to enliven the monotony of everyday life, the children are tempted to join in the fun and let their imaginations run riot. This may well have been the case. However, we cannot altogether shut our eyes to the fact that this peculiar sensitiveness of young children to phantom appearances is often alleged. In the case before us, the ready credulity of all concerned, and of the father in particular, is a very conspicuous element in the story, and the children are quick to take advantage of such a disposition in their elders.

eleven

Signed statement by an RIC Sergeant

This alleged account occurred somewhere in the vicinity of Old Connaught, located about three miles from Bray Town in County Wicklow. These alleged happenings come from the pen of an RIC sergeant who was stationed in Bray barracks in the year 1916. I give the following account from his signed statement:

I was a sergeant in the RIC in charge of a sub-district in or about November 1916. I had an official document which required the signature of a certain farmer in my district. Being on duty in the market-town on a Fair Day, I happened to meet the farmer on the street, and told him to call at my station at his earliest convenience to sign the document in question. The farmer replied saying, 'Sergeant, I am in great trouble. I came to town to-day to arrange for the funeral of my youngest child. I am suffering terrible annoyance in my house night and day for almost a week. Some unseen spirit is wrecking my house, throwing cooking utensils about and breaking delf. It flung a bottle of ink over my dying child, hurled a heavy glass salt-cellar at a mirror in the sick-room and broke a valuable tea set of old china that my wife was carrying downstairs for safety. She was about half way down the stairs with the china in her apron when the whole lot was completely smashed in my presence as well as in that of a few friends who had come to the wake. The day previous to the death of the child, myself and servants were churning in the kitchen, when the butter was taken from the churn and some of it thrown against the ceiling ten feet high. I found some of the broken china in my byre some thirty yards distant.'

I sympathised with the farmer, who was a strong active man, aged about forty. He had a farm of twelve acres or so, kept thirty cows, with two horses, young cattle and some sheep. He usually employed a manservant as well as a maid, and appeared to be in comfortable circumstances. His two-storied house, with eight or ten rooms, had a wide hall and a large kitchen. The entrance to the kitchen from the back door was along a passage across which a wall had been built to keep the draught from affecting the kitchen fire, as may be seen in most houses in Ireland.

I told the farmer not to come to the Barracks as it was three miles distant from where he lived, and that I would call on him at his house the day after the funeral. In accordance with this arrangement I went there a day or two later, and was shown the damage done, which was being added to hourly. I saw the butter, some of which was still on the ceiling, and went into the bedroom, a large room, in which the child died. I was shown the mirror which was hit exactly in the centre with such force as to leave a mark like the bottom of a salt-cellar. The mirror-glass was broken in a thousand streaks radiating from the point of injury. It was a good-quality dressing table and the mirror attached was of the heavy bevelled glass kind.

Having seen all the damage, I sat down in the kitchen in the presence of the farmer, his wife, two children (a boy about seven and a girl about ten) and the servant maid. I was adding some words to the document I had brought, when the little girl drew her mother's attention to a towel or kitchen-cloth being thrown across the kitchen towards the legs of the table near where I was seated. Whereupon the wife said, 'Maybe you'll believe it now, Sergeant.' Being engaged in writing I had not noticed anything and said so. The document having been signed, I listened to a full account the farmer gave me, in the presence of his family and servant, of the strange things which had been happening. The most striking part of the story was that the spook seemed to single out the wife and the little girl for all the punishment; the man himself was in no way molested. Although it was not more that 2.30p.m., being an old warrior, I was still unsatisfied with what I saw, and I came to the conclusion in my own mind that if some one of the seven or eight flitches of bacon that were suspended near the ceiling, or if one of the two horse-collars which were hanging on pins on the wall over the fireplace should be thrown down, I should then be satisfied as to the reality of the spook; but I took care not to betray what was passing in my mind, either by look or otherwise, to anybody that were present.

After addressing a few words to the wife about her making restitution, I stood up to go. The woman and children said they would not remain when I left, so they started for the back door, the servant first, followed by the two children, then the farmer's wife, next the farmer and I bringing up the rear. I had got across the kitchen near the end of the obstructing wall and was turning into the passage, but still in full view of the kitchen, when suddenly one of the horse-collars was flung from its position, high up on the wall, the whole length of the room, landing on the floor with a smack. The farmer turned and after we had both examined the collar, he said, 'You must now believe,' to which I assented. We passed into the yard, going towards the road, when a graip [dung-fork] was thrown across the yard by unseen hands.

These people were Catholics, and I advised the farmer to have Mass said in his house. Some days later I learned that the curate had said Mass there, and that even while Mass was being said there was some disturbance. I was further informed that immediately after my departure, the wife, children and servant sought shelter in the house of a neighbour. They were pursued by an unseen agent and pelted with turf and stones right up to the door. Much later, after I had left the RIC, I was told that the farmer had had to build a new dwelling at some distance from the original residence. The belief in the neighbourhood was that some time before this date, a man, who believed he had suffered a grievous wrong vowed to have revenge on the farmer's wife and her child. It was said that he lost his life in America just about the time the disturbances commenced. (Signed E.O'C.)

NOTES

There was a retired RIC Sergeant who lived in Lauderdale Terrace in Newtown Vevay, Bray, County Wicklow in 1919 who answered to the same initials.

twelve

Chaos at Court Street

The incidents related in the following story are taken from a paper read by Professor Barrett FRS, before the Society for Psychical Research. He made every possible inquiry into the facts set forth, short of being an eyewitness to the phenomena.

In the year 1910, there was a family named Redmond living in a house in Court Street, Enniscorthy. Mr Redmond was a labouring man. His wife took in lodgers to supplement her husband's income. At the time of these happenings there were three men boarding with them.

The house consisted of five rooms – two on the ground floor, of which one was a shop and the other a kitchen. The bedroom in which the boarders slept was large and contained two beds, one at each end of the room, two men sleeping in one of them, but the name of the third man is unknown – he seem to have left shortly after the disturbances began. The two other upstairs rooms were occupied by the Redmonds and their servant respectively.

It was on 4 July 1910, that John Randall, a carpenter, and George Sinnott took up residence in Redmonds. Later, in a signed statement now in the possession of Professor Barrett, John Randall tells a graphic tale of what occurred each night during the three weeks he lodged in the house, and how, as a result of the nightly disturbance, he lost three-quarters of a stone in weight.

It was on the night of Thursday 7 July that the first incident occurred, when the bedclothes were gently pulled off his bed. Of course he naturally thought it was a joke, and shouted to his companions to stop. As no one could explain what was happening, a match was struck, and the bedclothes were found to be at the window, from which the other bed (a large piece of furniture which ordinarily took two people to move) had been rolled when the clothes had been taken off Randall's bed. Things were put straight and the light was put out. Randall's account goes on to say:

It wasn't long before we heard tapping in the room. This lasted for a few minutes, getting quicker and quicker. When it got very quick, their bed moved across the room. We then struck a match and got the lamp. We searched the room thoroughly, and could find nobody. Nobody had come in the door. We called the man of the house [Redmond]; he came into the room, saw the bed, and told us to push it back and get into bed. (He thought that one of us was playing a trick on the other.) I said that I wouldn't stay in the other bed by myself, so I got in with the others; we put out the light again, and it had only been a couple of minutes and the bed ran out on the floor with the three of us. Redmond struck a match again, and this time we all got up and put on our clothes; we had got a terrible fright and couldn't stick it any longer. We told the man of the house we would sit up in the room till daylight. During the time we were sitting in the room we could hear footsteps leaving the kitchen and coming up the stairs; they would stop on the landing outside the door, and wouldn't come into the room. The footsteps and noises continued through the house until daybreak.

The next night the footsteps and noises were continued, but the unfortunate men did not experience any other annoyance. On the following day the men went home. They returned on the Sunday, and from that night till they finally left the house they were disturbed practically every night.

On Monday 11 July, the bed was continually running out from the wall with its three occupants. They kept the lamp alight, and a chair was seen to dance out onto the middle of the floor. On the following Thursday, we read of the same happenings, with the addition that one of the boarders was lifted out of the bed, though he felt no hand near him. It seems strange that they should have gone through such a bad night exactly a week from the night the poltergeist started its operations. So the account goes on; every night that they slept in the room the haunting continued, some nights being worse than others:

On Friday, 29th July, the bed turned up on one side and threw us out on the floor, and before we were thrown out, the pillows were taken from under my head three times. When the bed rose up, it fell back without making any noise. This bed was so heavy, it took both the women and the girl to pull it out from the wall without anybody in it, and there were only three castors on it. The men took refuge in the other bed. They had not been long in it before it began to rise, but could not be got out of the recess it was in unless it was taken to pieces.

A Mr Murphy, from the Guardian office, and another man named Devereux, came and stopped in the room one night. The experiences of Murphy and Devereux are contained in a further statement, signed by Murphy and collaborated by Devereux.

They seemed to have gone to work in a business-like manner, as, before taking their positions for the night, they made a complete investigation of the bedroom and house, so as to eliminate all chance of trickery or fraud. By this time, it should be noted, one of Mrs Redmond's lodgers had evidently suffered enough from the poltergeist, as only two men are mentioned in Murphy's statement, one sleeping in each bed. The two investigators took up their position against the wall midway between the two beds, so that they had a full view of the room and the occupants of the beds. 'The night', says Murphy, 'was a clear starlight night. No blind obstructed the view from outside, and one could see the outlines of the beds and their occupants clearly. At about 11.30p.m. a tapping was

_ to the foot of Randall's bed. 'My companion remarked that
_d to be like the noise of a rat eating at timber.' Sinnott replied,
oon see the rat it is.'

tapping went on slowly at first, then the speed gradually increased
to 100 or 120 per minute, the noise growing louder. This continued for
about five minutes, and then it stopped suddenly. Randall then spoke.
He said, 'The clothes are slipping off my bed. Look at them sliding off.
Good God, they are going off me.' Mr Devereux immediately struck
a match, which he already had in his hand. The bedclothes had partly
left the boy's bed, having gone diagonally towards the foot, going out
at the left corner, and not alone did they seem to be drawn off the bed,
but they appeared to be actually going back under the bed, much in the
same position one would expect bedclothes to be if a strong breeze were
blowing through the room at the time. But then everything was calm. A
search was then made for wires or strings, but nothing of the sort could
be found. The bedclothes were put back and the light extinguished. For
ten minutes there was silence, only to be broken by more rapping which
was followed by shouts by Randall. He was told to hold on to the clothes,
which were sliding off again. But this was of little use, for he was heard to
cry, 'I'm going', and when the light was struck he was seen to slide from
the bed and all the bedclothes with him. Randall, who, with Sinnott,
had shown considerable strength of mind by staying in the house under
such trying circumstances, had evidently had enough, for as he lay on the
floor, trembling in every limb and bathed in perspiration, he exclaimed,
'Oh isn't this dreadful? I can't stand it; I can't stay here any longer.' He
was eventually persuaded to get back into bed. Later on, more rapping
occurred in a different part of the room, but it soon stopped, and the rest
of the night passed away in peace.

Randall and Sinnott went to their homes the next day, and Mr
Murphy spent from eleven till long past midnight in their vacated room,
but heard and saw nothing unusual. He stated in conclusion, 'Randall
could not reach that part of the floor from which the rapping came on
any occasion without attracting my attention and that of my partners.'

thirteen

Something to Hide

In the early sixties, in the city of Dublin, a building that had once housed a firm of solicitors was being renovated. When the workmen reached the cellar they discovered some very old safes used in times gone by for storing wills and deeds to properties. Since the firm had long been defunct, no keys could be found and the safes had to be blown – thousands of wills and other papers belonging to people long since departed were taken and destroyed. Two workmen had taken home some very old wills and other papers; it was from these papers that one of them found this signed statement by the Rector of the parish of C. in County Wicklow.

What is interesting about this case is that an exorcism was carried out by a Rector of the Church of Ireland. In most cases of haunting, or in cases of demonic possession, it is usually a Catholic priest who is called. Another feature that impressed me was that the people were reluctant to give their names, which proves that they were not out to seek publicity, and the fact that the document was hidden away in a solicitor's safe further testifies to the integrity of the people involved.

In 1871, the late Mr H. came to reside at Y. From time to time noises were heard in certain rooms in the old part of the house, footsteps and sounds as if people were conversing. Mr H. frequently attempted to discover the cause of these disturbances, but in vain, and for fifteen years afterwards, when his daughter Miss H. resided in the house, often alone, sounds such as the slamming of doors and the tramping of footsteps up and down the room would be heard. But there would be long periods when no disturbance was detected.

In 1913, there was a recurrence of these sounds. In 1922 and 1923, the noises grew worse. A Miss G.M., who came to reside at Y. and knew nothing of these disturbances, complained at the opening and shutting of doors, knockings at the front door and bedroom doors. She related that she would sometimes waken at night and feel the presence of something evil near her. Other people who had stayed at the house had the same experience. In December 1924, things came to a head. There were knockings, opening and slamming of doors. They related that night and day there was a barrage of noises that never ceased and almost drove them frantic with terror. During this terrible period there were no servants in the house, only the two ladies in question and a woman who came in two nights a week to help them.

In January Miss G.H. contacted me with a view to holding a service of exorcism in the house, which he did on Tuesday, January the 13th at 9a.m. The service took the form of certain prayers read from the services appointed in the Priest's Prayer-Book for blessing a house, preceded by a celebration of Holy Communion, special prayers were also used for protection from evil spirits, and for the repose of the souls of any in an unhappy condition. Since the holding of the service there has been no recurrence of these unpleasant noises and happenings, nor has there been perceived the strange presence of an evil personality, which had been felt by Miss G.H. and Miss G.M. and others.
(Signed) B.A. Rector of C.
County Wicklow
We have read the foregoing, and declare that it is a true statement of the facts of the case.
(Signed) G.H.   G.M.

NOTES
This may have been in Carnew, South Wicklow.

Conclusion

When Oscar Wilde was serving out his sentence in Reading Gaol, he was once approached by a fellow inmate who told him that he suspected that the prison was haunted and wanted to know what Mr Wilde thought. Wilde was adament, 'No! You see my dear fellow, prisons have no tradition. If you wish to witness such phenomenon you must go instead to a stately home where the ghost is inherited along with the family jewels.'

The romantic image of a ghost gliding at the stroke of midnight down the corridor of some old mansion is one that has persisted in the public imagination. The reverse is the truth. You are more likely to witness this phenomenon in a housing estate than you are in the Tower of London. There is nothing romantic about these manifestations; they sometimes cause havoc to the lives of the unfortunate inhabitants and in most cases the priest has to be called in to exorcise the house, sometimes with negative results.

There are recorded cases of people having to flee their homes, causing hardship and stress on both children and parents, devaluation of their property and the psychological terror that attends it.

Down through the ages, all documented investigation into alleged poltergeist activity was, and still is, based on the credibility of the person or persons involved. In the past, people were brought before the courts, both civil and ecclesiastical, to swear a solemn oath as to the truth of their testimony that neither trickery nor any other form of deceit was involved.

In the case of children, this remains a contentious problem. It is a well-known fact that in many, if not all of alleged poltergeist activity, young girls have somehow mysteriously been the medium by which these dramas were played out. Those engaged in the investigations of these alleged happenings have been on the whole people of position and of the highest character, people trained to detect trickery and deception. Notwithstanding this, even the most diligent have been deceived into believing what turned out to be deception of the most subtle nature; hence lies the horns of this dilemma. Only the most astute, after sifting all of the evidence (disclaiming all hearsay knowledge or the giving of evidence after a long period of time) will then render a verdict. Here it must be stated that there are thousands of such alleged cases that have passed every conceivable test as to render them as happenings not yet within the scope of human understanding and until then must remain by their very nature mysterious and unexplainable. To approach the subject from any rational viewpoint is an exercise in futility. Regarding such phenomena I am the most skeptical of beings. G.K. Chesterton once remarked that the most uncommon quality was plain common sense. So let us briefly and calmly turn the spotlight on the few aforementioned cases in the light of common day and not in that sphere where things go bump in the night.

How often have we heard someone say, 'That house is not haunted? I know people who lived in the same house for years and never heard a thing?' It doesn't work that way.

Take the case of the cottage on the Convent Hill in Bray. I knew the family that lived there for nearly forty years. The same cottage that Mick Healy and his family fled from within the space of a month. Why would a man who was offered the job of a life time in the hungry thirties pack up and go, to where? To what?

Now take the case near Old Connaught. Anybody who has ever worked for or had any dealings with farmers will testify to the fact that when it comes to money they are not readily forecoming, unless it is to their own advantage. It is ludicrous to even suggest that this farmer in question would be compelled to build a new dwelling if what had happened was not of a violent and terrifying nature and not the pranks of children.

Take the landlady in Enniscorthy who took in journeymen lodgers which afforded her with a welcome added source of income. Why would she or any of her family conceive a story that not only drove lodgers away but brought a very unwelcome source of attention to her dwelling as news reached the national newspapers, resulting in a lengthy inquiry? The alleged happenings in question were proven to have happened and could not have been the result of any form of fraud or trickery. Twenty years ago a man I knew in Newtownmountkennedy (Noël, sadly deceased) told me of an ordeal that he and two other men had endured in a house they had lodged in in Enniscorthy. This had been the same dwelling where these alleged happenings had occurred eighty years before. He knew nothing of the history of that house and what had occurred there all those years before.

Such stories are legion and as yet unexplained. What have I learned in writing these short accounts? That there are things that happen that are as yet out of the scope of our understanding. Maybe it's time that our scientists took off the blinkers and their tunnelled view of the world and took a hard look at what has been happening in our universe for possibly as long as we have peopled the earth and will continue to do so until the stars go out.